ALL THE PAINTINGS OF
BOTTICELLI

Part 4

VOLUME TWENTY-EIGHT
in the
Complete Library of World Art

The Complete Library of World Art

ALL THE PAINTINGS

OF BOTTICELLI

Part 4 (1485–1510)

Text by ROBERTO SALVINI

Translated from the Italian by
JOHN GRILLENZONI

HAWTHORN BOOKS, INC.
Publishers · New York

*Printed and bound in Great Britain by
Jarrold & Sons Ltd., Norwich*

CONTENTS

	page
BOTTICELLI'S PAINTINGS (*continued*)	151
LOST PAINTINGS	171
PAINTINGS ATTRIBUTED TO BOTTICELLI	173
LOCATION OF PAINTINGS	185
SELECTED CRITICISM	189
BIBLIOGRAPHICAL NOTE	197
REPRODUCTIONS	203

BOTTICELLI'S PAINTINGS

Color Plate I

ST. AUGUSTINE IN HIS CELL.
Detail of plate 59.

Plate 61

PORTRAIT OF LORENZO LOREN-
ZANO. *Panel, 49 × 37.** Philadelphia,
John G. Johnson Collection.* From the
Lazzaroni Collection in Paris, it went
to the Johnson Collection, and then
to its present location. L. Dorez
published it in 1907, and A. Venturi
in 1908; it is generally accepted as
autograph. An inscription in the
upper part of the portrait identifies
the sitter as Lorenzano. He was a
Florentine scholar belonging to the
Medici circle and was professor of
dialectic at the University of Pisa in
1479, then professor of physics in
1482. In 1487, he became professor
of medicine. He was close to Pietro
Crinito, Pico della Mirandola and
even Savonarola. He committed
suicide in 1502. We cannot date the
painting from Lorenzano's age,
because we do not know when he
was born. We accept Berenson's
dating of 1490 on the basis of the
comparison of this portrait with the
heads of the saints in the *Coronation*
in the Uffizi (other critics agreeing:
Bode, A. and L. Venturi, Van Marle,
Gamba, Mesnil, Bettini). Yashiro's
dating of 1487 (about) is not as likely.

Plate 62

PORTRAIT OF MARULLUS. *Transferred to canvas, 49 × 35. Barcelona,
Cambó Collection.* In the nineteenth

century, it belonged to the Duke of
Leuchtenberg in Petersburg. On a
panel, the painting was larger and
almost square in shape (*Katalog Slg.
Leuchtenberg*, Berlin, 1851), and was
attributed to Masaccio, and later to
Filippino. In 1906, it was acquired
by the Simon Collection in Berlin,
and attributed to Botticelli by F.
Laban and then by Bode. The later
dating preferred by Kroeger and
Bode, that is, around 1485–90, has
proved more correct than the earlier
dates proposed by A. Venturi
(around the time of the Roman
frescoes, 1481) and by Van Marle
(close to the *St Sebastian*, 1474), ever
since Berenson identified the sitter as
the Greek humanist Michael Marullo,
called the *Tarcaniota*. Croce supported Berenson (*Michele Marullo...*,
1938). Marullo was born in 1453,
and was a professor in Naples when
he was invited to Florence in 1489 by
Pierfrancesco de' Medici. He remained until 1494, and then returned
in 1496 to marry the poetess
Alessandra Scala. The sitter's age,
certainly less than forty, demon-
strates that the portrait was painted
during his first visit to Florence,
around 1490 or soon after. I do not
agree with Gamba and Bettini that
there is evidence of *bottega* work, nor
do I agree with Gamba in dating it
around 1500.

Plate 63

MADONNA AND CHILD WITH ST
JOHN THE BAPTIST. *Canvas, 134 ×
92. Florence, Pitti Palace.* Morelli

* All dimensions are in centimeters.

151

rejected the traditional attribution carried in the old inventories (in *Gazette des Beaux-Arts*, 1886) and declared it a workshop product. A. Venturi agreed (1925) and later Berenson (1932), considered it a copy of a lost work. Gamba and Mesnil also accepted Morelli's thesis. Ulmann (1893), Bode (1921 and 1926) and Schmarsow (1923) consider it authentic, Bettini (1942) who emphatically states: ". . . only Botticelli —in a moment of full lyric consciousness—could have created the strange, involuted, closed lines of the Pitti *Madonna* . . ." As for dating it, everyone agrees it is a late work, and furthermore it should be noted that the Uffizi *Annunciation* provides a point of departure (plate 38), because the Virgin repeats the essential lines of the *Annunciation* but complicates them in a tormented fashion. The painting dates, therefore, from 1490–95, as Bode already has said, while Schmarsow insists on a later date, around 1500.

Plate 64

NATIVITY. *Drawing, 16 × 26. Florence, Uffizi.* Pen, watercolor, and lead highlights on prepared rose paper. Traditionally ascribed to Botticelli, it was reascribed to his school and Lorenzo di Credi's by Morelli, but Berenson, Bode, Yashiro, Van Marle, Gamba and Bertini confirmed tradition. Despite the broad resemblance to the *Mystic Nativity* in London (plate 114), it is rightly considered earlier (that is, around 1491) by Yashiro and Bertini. We would say it was close to the *Lamentation* in Munich (plate 65) and the one in Milan (plate 66).

Plate 65

PIETÀ. *Panel, 110 × 207. Munich, Alte Pinakothek.* Acquired in Florence in 1815 for the hereditary prince, Louis of Bavaria, it became the property of the state in 1850. Mesnil discovered that it was originally located in the Church of San Paolino. In fact, a *Pietà* of that size which had come from the convent of San Paolino is included in the list of paintings that Luigi Scotti restored at the Uffizi in 1813. The identification frequently attempted with the *Pietà* Vasari records in Santa Maria Maggiore is thus disproved, and Horne rejected it earlier simply because of its size. Many critics consider it autograph, but Berenson, Horne, Van Marle and Mesnil consider it a workshop product. Like the *Lamentation* in Milan (plate 66), of which this painting is often considered a prototype, it is to be judged substantially autograph, even if the workshop collaborated (under the master's supervision). The date oscillates between 1490 and 1500. The typological relationships of the saints to those in the *Coronation* in the Uffizi (plate 42) makes a date later than 1490 more probable.

Plate 66

PIETÀ. *Panel, 107 × 71. Milan, Poldi-Pezzoli Museum.* This was acquired in 1855 as a Botticelli, and Bertini confirmed the attribution in his catalog of 1881. In the second edition of his *Lives,* Vasari tells us that "in Santa Maria Maggiore in Florence there is a lovely *Pietà* with small figures at the side of the Panciatichi Chapel." This *Pietà* is still registered in the sacristy of the church by Richa in 1755. Since the panel was "at the side" of the chapel, it must have hung on a pilaster and therefore have been oblong in shape. Several scholars, especially Van Hadeln (1906), have thus argued that this is the same panel as the one mentioned by Vasari. Others, however, think that the panel now in Munich is the one Vasari referred to (plate 65), but that seems improbable since the panel is wide. Horne, on the other hand, considers both this panel in the Poldi-Pezzoli Museum and the one which up to 1904 was in the Bourgeois Collection in Cologne and then in the Bautier Collection in Brussels (plate 150) as copies of the Santa Maria Maggiore panel, which is lost. The identity of the painting is a question linked with its author. Morelli, Frizzoni, Horne, Berenson, A. and L. Venturi and Mesnil tend to consider it a workshop product or a copy of the Munich panel or of the now lost original. Even though admitting some assistance, Ulmann, Bode, Schmarsow, Van Marle, Gamba, Bettini, Russoli (1955) and Argan argue that it is Botticelli's work. The high quality of the work, which is apparent after Pellicoli cleaned it in 1951, confirms that it is substantially autograph. Critics date the panel between about 1490 and 1500. The fact that we can discern a certain pathos characteristic of Savonarola does not, in itself, mean that we must date the panel at the time of the friar's execution—especially since he had held sway in Florence ever since 1490. On the other hand, the still strong plastic formation of the figures point to a moment close to the *Coronation* in the Uffizi (plate 42), so that we would venture a dating of around 1492–94. The *Lamentation* in Munich probably follows chronologically, not because it derives from this painting, but because it seems a more successful resolution of the same theme in the upward development of the composition.

Plate 67

PIETÀ. Detail: the head of a pious woman and Christ.

Plate 68

ST THOMAS. *Drawing, 17·5 × 12. Milan, Ambrosiana (Resta Ms., folio 19).* Pen with lead highlights on a pencil sketch; tinted paper. This is traditionally attributed and accepted by Berenson, Yashiro, Van Marle, Gamba and Bertini (1953). It served for the print of the *Assumption*. Certainly later than 1490.

Plate 69

THE LAST COMMUNION OF ST JEROME. *Panel, 33 × 35. New York, Metropolitan Museum of Art.* From the collection of Gino Capponi in Florence (Fantozzi, *Guida di Firenze*, 1844), where it was attributed to Andrea del Castagno, it went to his heirs, the Marchesi Farinola. In 1915, it was part of the Altman Bequest to the Metropolitan. Cavenaghi cleaned it shortly before 1908. Bode at first considered it a copy of a similar painting in Palazzo Balbi in Genoa, which he attributed to Filippino Lippi. Morelli later ascribed it to Botticelli and his opinion is now generally accepted. Another old copy came from the Abdy Collection in Paris, and now exists in a private American collection. A "*St Jerome receiving communion*" is mentioned in the inventory (1492) of Lorenzo the Magnificent's collection, while a "St Jerome, a singular work" is recorded in the *Anonimo Gaddiano* among Botticelli's small works, but any identification of this panel with any of those described in these sources is uncertain. Horne's suggestion seems more likely; that is, that this was the "*Transition of St Jerome*" by the hand of Sandro

Botticelli," which Francesco del Pugliese left, along with four other paintings, to the chapel of the castle in Sommaia. He had acquired the castle in 1488, and had made provision to bestow it to the friars of San Marco in case his family should be left without heirs (but in a later testament, the entire inheritance went to his cousin Niccolò di Piero del Pugliese). Horne showed that the theme is taken from an apocryphal letter by St Eusebius, printed in Venice and in Messina in 1473 and in Florence in 1490. The dating varies between about 1490 and 1500. The fact that the tension of the line is still united to a firm plastic structure in the figures would seem to indicate a date later than 1490, but not much more so. Close in time to the *Lamentation* in Munich (plate 65) and the one in Milan (plate 66).

Plate 70

(UNFINISHED) ADORATION OF THE MAGI. *Panel, 107·5 × 173. Florence, Uffizi*. Drawn and sketched in chiaroscuro with bistre on a ground, then partially colored, it seems, in the seventeenth century. It was acquired by the Uffizi on April 20, 1779 as a Botticelli, and first exhibited in 1880. Since 1940, it has been in storage. Commented on by Heath Wilson (in *The Academy*, November 20, 1880), who believed he could detect the portraits of Lorenzo the Magnificent, Savonarola Benivieni and Leonardo. He considered the painting to be autograph and a late work. F. O. Schulze considered it by a late follower. Ulmann and Ridolfi also thought it was a late work. Ulmann identified it with the "story of the three Magi in the Palazzo Signoria, over the stairs which lead to the Catena" described in the *Anonimo Gaddiano*, but Horne

was quick to point out that all evidence indicates that the scene in the Palazzo was a fresco. Picking up the idea proposed by Müller-Walde and Müntz of a possible case of Leonardo's influence, Ridolfi thought this painting was inspired by Leonardo's incomplete *Adoration*. Bettini recently revived the possibility that Botticelli was influenced by Leonardo on the latter's return from Milan around 1500, not only in this *Adoration*, but also in the *Transfiguration* (plate 147) and in the *Pentecost* in Greenville (plate 148). Horne believed he could discern some Pollaiuolo touches and explained the similarities with the Leonardo as Botticelli's influence on Leonardo, since, he argued, the style of this *Adoration* could only belong to the period around 1480, before Botticelli left for Rome. But with the exception of Horne and Yashiro, most of the critics agree it is a late work and date it around 1500. While I frankly do not see appreciable similarities with Leonardo, except for some hint of *sfumato* resulting from the seventeenth-century repainting, I do think that the grand and passionate movement which engulfs the still solid figures signals the stylistic phase between the *Coronation* (plate 42) and *Calumny* (plates 92–93), and so I would date it around 1492–93.

Plate 71a

(UNFINISHED) ADORATION OF THE MAGI. Detail: the group near the Virgin.

Plate 71b

ADORATION OF THE MAGI (FRAGMENT). *Central section, canvas, 30 × 23. Cambridge, Fitzwilliam Museum*. Along with the fragments reproduced in plates 72–73, this section formed an *Adoration of the Magi*, drawn and then shaded in tempera on canvas. Plate 73 is made up of two pieces, of which the larger was published and attributed to Filippino Lippi by W. Young Ottley (1823). With the other pieces, it was part of the Russell Collection at Onslow Gardens until 1884. When the collection was sold, it went to the Knowles Collection, and from there (1908) to the Clough Collection in London. The fragment in plate 71b went to the Brough Collection in Stafford, and the one in plate 72 to the Salting Collection, where Ulmann saw it in 1893 and judged it an autograph Botticelli. It then went to the Fairfax Murray Collection. The smaller section appeared in 1896 at a sale at Sotheby's, and Clough himself bought it to go with the other piece (1908). Horne rejected the attribution to Botticelli, and judged it a copy of the *Adoration* the *Anonimo Gaddiano* described in the Palazzo Vecchio. But Yashiro reopened the question, and his attribution was accepted by Berenson and Bertini. Generally held to be contemporary with or later than the *Madonna and Child* in Washington (plate 60), it would seem more related to the incomplete *Adoration* in the Uffizi (plate 70). It even appears that these fragments are only a variation of that *Adoration*.

Plate 72

ADORATION OF THE MAGI (FRAGMENT). *Left side, canvas, 17·5 × 19·5. New York, Pierpont Morgan Library.* Cf. comment on plate 71b.

Plate 73

THE ADORATION OF THE MAGI (FRAGMENT). *Right side, canvas, 44 × 37. Cambridge, Fitzwilliam Museum.* Cf. comment on plate 71b.

DRAWINGS FOR THE DIVINE COMEDY

Plates 74–86

Vasari claims that as soon as he had returned from Rome after finishing the frescoes in the Sistine Chapel, Botticelli "commented on a part of Dante because he was a learned person, and he drew figures from the *Inferno* and printed them. He spent a great amount of time on this and so without working (for money) he had to face many difficulties." Apart from the "commentary" of which no trace exists (perhaps Vasari was being fanciful), Vasari is referring to the preliminary drawings for the *Divine Comedy*, now lost, which were badly reproduced by engraving for the 1481 edition of the poem with commentary by Cristoforo Landini. Baccio Baldini probably did the engravings, since Vasari described him elsewhere (in the *Life* of Raimondi) as Botticelli's engraver because "Botticelli had not drawn much." The description concerns some illustrations for the first nineteen cantos of the *Inferno*, and the work, we can imagine, was left unfinished because Botticelli was called to Rome in 1481 (and since the Landini edition was published in 1481, Vasari's chronology is mistaken). But Vasari does recall that Botticelli spent some time on the drawings, and here we detect a confused recollection of another illustration from Dante, also incomplete but much more extensive, which consists of ninety-three drawings now in the Staatliche Museen in Berlin and in the Vatican Museums. In fact, the *Anonimo Gaddiano* tells us that Botticelli "painted and illustrated Dante on parchment for Lorenzo di Pierfrancesco de' Medici, which was held to be a marvelous thing."

The greater part of these drawings, which were probably scattered even during Vasari's time, reappeared in a codex in the Duke of Hamilton's collection in Glasgow, which he had acquired in 1803 from the Paris bookseller, Claude Molini. Waagen was the first to mention the codex (1854) and although he did not know the passage from the *Anonimo Gaddiano*, which Milanesi cited in his notes on Vasari (1878), he recognized Botticelli's hand but he attributed the series as a whole to various artists of differing caliber. Lippmann acquired the codex along with the entire Hamilton library in 1882 for the Berlin Museums. Lippmann immediately published the drawings, and other reviews appeared, by Rosenberg and by Epherussi (1885–86). In 1886, several pages that had been missing from the Hamilton codex were found by Strzygowsk, in an odd volume in the Vatican Library (left as part of Christina of Sweden's bequest to Pope Alexander VII in 1689; the illustrations were already noted by De Batines in his *Bibliografia dantesca*, but he did not detect Botticelli's hand). Cf. also Pératé, in *Gazette des Beaux-Arts*, 1887. The recto of each parchment folio carries the text of a canto in four columns in excellent fifteenth-century calligraphy. On the reverse side is the drawing for the next canto so as to face the text in book form, except for Canto XXXXIV, which has two: one of the usual size, the other on two sheets joined together. Executed in silverpoint and lead (many were done over in pen and then the sketch was scratched), the drawings were obviously intended to be colored as miniatures. Luckily only four—and these partially—were so colored, by someone almost certainly other than Botticelli: the map of the *Inferno*, and the illustrations for Cantos X, XV and XVIII of the *Inferno* (in the first, just the robes of Dante and Virgil have been done in tempera). Two of the drawings (*Inferno*, Canto XXX and *Purgatorio*, Canto VIII) were left as metal point sketches, along with parts of others. Some others from the *Paradiso* were left incomplete even as sketches. The drawings were scattered; to the Vatican, the map of the *Inferno*, with the illustration to the first canto on the reverse side, and the illustrations to Cantos IX, X, XII, XIII, XV, XVI. To Berlin, the Kupferstich-kabinett, the illustrations for Cantos VIII, XVII–XXXIV of the *Inferno*, all thirty-three of the *Purgatorio* drawings (with the map related to Canto I), and all the drawings for *Paradiso*, except for Canto XXX and Canto XXXIII, represented by blank pages. Thus along with these two, the illustrations to Cantos II, III, IV, V, VI, VII, XI and XIV of the *Inferno* were missing.

In 1939, the drawings in Berlin were put in safe storage—some in the east, others in western Germany. After the war only a few of the drawings in West Germany, where most had been kept, were found. There are now only three in the Staatliche Museen in Berlin: Cantos XXIX and XXXI of the *Inferno*, and Canto III of the *Purgatorio*. The rest are probably in Russia. For more details, and for an exact description of the series, in relation to the text of the poem and even to the engravings for the Landini edition, cf. Horne, 1908; for recent events, cf. Y. Batard, *Les Dessins de Sandro Botticelli pour la Divine Comédie*, 1952.

No one except Waagen has ever doubted the attribution to Botticelli, who signed the series besides, on the tablet carried by the smallest angel in the illustration to Canto XXVIII of the *Paradiso*. Horne reads it "Sandro di Mariano," while A. Venturi claims it is more of an artist's signature, reading "Sandro di sua mano" (Sandro by his hand).

As to dating the series, Horne's careful study of the biography and political fortunes of the patron, Lorenzo di Pierfrancesco, shows, I think irrefutably, that the work was interrupted when Lorenzo had to flee Florence at the end of March, 1497. Botticelli must have been on friendly terms with Lorenzo at least until 1496, because Michelangelo addressed a letter to him in care of Botticelli from Rome, apparently because he feared interception by Lorenzo's enemies. But later, certainly, the artist's relations with Lorenzo must have grown quite cool. Lorenzo and his brother Giovanni had opposed the government of their cousin Piero de' Medici, and were arrested on April 24, 1494 and confined to their villas in Castello and Cefaggiolo under indictment of having plotted against their cousin with the King of France. They fled, but returned to Florence with the amnesty decreed under Charles VIII. They took sides with Pier Capponi and called themselves "*popolani*" (of the people) and were associated with Savonarola's republican movement. But they soon showed signs of wanting to replace their cousins as rulers of Florence, now that the other Medicis were in exile. They must have had an open argument with the "criers" (Savonarola's followers), because they were compelled to leave the city, accused of plotting against the republic with the Duke of Milan. After 1496, Lorenzo and Giovanni probably headed the *compagnacci* (the bad companions), as we learn from

Simone Botticelli's (Sandro's brother diary, in describing the assault on San Marco and the capture of Savonarola by the band instigated by Giovanni.

I think it improbable, therefore, that Botticelli continued to work for his old patron after these events. If Botticelli was not directly involved with the "criers" he was definitely sympathetic. In 1501, he signed a painting with an apocalyptic epigraph inspired by Savonarola's teachings (cf. comment on plate 114).

I would say that the drawings were begun not earlier than 1490, because the first among them correspond stylistically to the *Coronation* in the Uffizi (plate 42), just as the last in order do not go beyond the period in which he did the *Calumny* (plates 92–93). He must have paused to do this work, therefore, between 1490 and 1496. A large selection from the series is published in the following plates.

Plate 74

CANTO I OF THE INFERNO. *Drawing, 47 × 32. Vatican City, Vatican Library.* There are several stains, and the drawing is faded. But the figures of Dante in the wood can easily be recognized. The figure is repeated twice, and we see him confronting the lion. Then we see him retreat before the wolf, while from the rocks appears the figure of Virgil.

Plate 75

CANTO IX OF THE INFERNO. *Drawing, 47 × 32. Vatican City, Vatican Library.* The upper part relates to the preceding canto: one can see the marsh of the Styx with the "muddy people"; on the right is Plegyas with his boat. In the lower part, on the left, are the two poets (the figures are repeated four times

157

to show the four incidents of the scene). An approach to the city of Dis is made, the threatening Furies stand on the tower while menacing demons appear at the entrance; the angel flies down from above and reappears in front of the door to admonish the demons. On the other side of the tower the poets appear again, surrounded by the burning tombs of the Heretics.

Plate 76

CANTO IX OF THE INFERNO. *Drawing, 47 × 32. Vatican City, Vatican Library.* Detail of the left side. At Virgil's behest, Dante takes a branch from the plant which contains the soul of Piero delle Vigne. The nude figure crouching at the right, pursued by dogs, and the other figure just below, illustrate the episode of Lano del Troppo and Giacomo da Santandrea. In front of Giacomo, Dante can be seen replacing the foliage of the Plant (soul) of Lotto degli Agli (or of Rocco de' Mozzi). Toward the centre, a harpy.

Color Plate II

CALUMNY. Detail of plates 92–93.

Plate 77

CANTO XXVI OF THE INFERNO. *Drawing, 47 × 32. Formerly in Berlin, Kupferstichkabinett.* Panorama of the eighth bowge, with the fires that burn the fraudulent counselors. Dante and Virgil emerge from the rocks. We see a third representation of the two poets, inspired by vv. 43–45—"I stood on the bridge looking underneath/if I had not grasped the rock/I would have fallen down without striking." The only allusion to the conversation with Ulysses and Diomedes is the divided

flame, at the tips of which are sketched the faces of the two Greeks.

Plate 78

CANTO XXIX OF THE INFERNO. *Drawing, 47 × 32. Berlin, Kupferstichkabinett.* The account begins at the upper left, where the two poets, still on the bridge which spans the bowge of the instigators of discord, face Bertran del Bornio, who, as the preceding canto describes him, carries his truncated head by the hair like a lantern, and Geri del Bello, who threatens Dante with his finger (XXIX, 25). On the right we can still see the many sufferings of the instigators. Further down, the two poets cross the bridge which spans the bowge of the counterfeiters. Below at the right, we can see Dante and Virgil at the foot of the bridge talking to the alchemists, Griffolino and Capocchio.

Plate 79

CANTO XXXI OF THE INFERNO. *Drawing, 47 × 32. Berlin, Kupferstichkabinett.* Detail: in the background the figures of the two poets. In the foreground, the giants: Nembrotte blowing the horn; at his right, taller and in chains, Fialte; the half-figure in front of him, also in chains, Briareo; and at the extreme right, we see Anteo bending over to pick up the two poets to put them in the next circle. At the left, in the foreground, two more giants.

Plate 80

CANTO III OF THE PURGATORIO. *Drawing, 47 × 32. Berlin, Kupferstichkabinett.* The upper center, the angel in the boat that has ferried the souls to Purgatory moves away. On the shore, we see five nude figures fleeing toward the mountain, after Cato's warning. Dante starts out with Virgil, and they arrive at the foot of the mountain, where the artist has drawn in a harsh flight of steps. Nearby, the poets are shown again, while the souls "with the backs of their hands" show them the way. The drawing is probably incomplete. (There is no clear indication of Manfredi.)

Plate 81

CANTO XI OF THE PURGATORIO. *Drawing, 47 × 32. Formerly in Berlin, Kupferstichkabinett.* The two poets appear three times as they pass through the gyre of the proud, who are shown bearing heavy loads. Dante can be seen in the center talking to Omberto Aldebrandesco, and at the left, with Oderisi da Gubbio. Drawing probably unfinished.

Plate 82

CANTO XXXIII OF THE PUR-GATORIO. *Drawing, 47 × 32. Formerly in Berlin, Kupferstichkabinett.* Detail: in the earthly paradise, the three theological Virtues and the four cardinal Virtues together with Matelda and Beatrice lead Dante and Statius to the River Eunoes.

Plate 83

CANTO I OF THE PARADISO. *Drawing, 47 × 32. Formerly in Berlin, Kupferstichkabinett.* Dante and Beatrice fly from the earthly paradise toward the *primum mobile*.

Plate 84

CANTO VI OF THE PARADISO. *Drawing, 47 × 32. Formerly in Berlin, Kupferstichkabinett.* Dante and Beatrice come to rest near Mercury, inhabited by the active spirits. Beatrice points out the "light" of Justinian, whose famous speech on the Roman eagle becomes the theme of this canto.

Plate 85

CANTO XXI OF THE PARADISO. *Drawing, 47 × 32. Formerly in Berlin, Kupferstichkabinett.* In the sky near Saturn, we see Dante and Beatrice before the celestial stairs, surrounded by the souls of the blessed, which the poet describes as "splendors" and the artist draws as small angels. On the stairs, Dante and Beatrice appear again, drawn only in silverpoint.

Plate 86

CANTO XXVII OF THE PARADISO. *Drawing, 47 × 32. Formerly in Berlin, Kupferstichkabinett.* Botticelli illustrates the eighth heaven with very light clouds. Below, Beatrice asks Dante to look at the earth beneath them (vv. 76 ff.). Above, Beatrice and Dante rise to the ninth heaven (vv. 97 ff.).

Plate 87

PORTRAIT OF DANTE. *Canvas, 54·5 × 47·5. Formerly in Hatfield, Burns Collection.* Until 1892, the painting was in the Seymour Collection in London; then it was in the Langton Douglas Collection until 1930. Mrs. Burns owned it until a few years ago, and we do not know who the new owner is. Bode attributed the *Portrait* to Botticelli verbally to Ulmann in 1893, and he confirmed it in 1921 and 1926. A. Venturi, Gamba, and Salmi also attribute it to the master. Kroeber and Mesnil doubt the attribution. Even though repainted, it is autograph, carried out in connection with the drawings from Dante, and probably dating from around 1495.

Plate 88

FAUN. *Drawing, 13·5 × 16. Florence, Uffizi.* Pen and bistre on white paper. Ferri published it as autograph, and related it to the illustrations for the

Divine Comedy (*Inferno*), but Berenson considered it a copy of Botticelli's drawing for the Zephyrs in the *Birth of Venus*, or as a completely reworked original. But these reservations seem entirely unjustified in the face of the drawing's quality, and in fact, Gamba and Bertini ascribe it to Botticelli. Rather than associating it with the *Birth of Venus*, I would prefer the drawings for the *Inferno*.

Plate 89

DERELITTA. *Panel, 46 × 42. Rome, Palavicini Collection.* Detail: the central part. This famous and baffling painting was purchased in Florence in 1816 by Prince Giuseppe Rospigliosi as a Masaccio. The figure was allegedly Rea Silvia. A. Venturi reclaimed it for Botticelli in 1896, and critics have generally agreed with his judgment. Antoniewicz attributed it to Filippino Lippi, Giorgio dello Hartlaub to Francesca, and Lesser to Ercole de' Roberti; there was some doubt, during the Italian show in London in 1930, whether the painting was a Pre-Raphaelite English product or not. As for the subject, there have been various interpretations, from the purely literary one of Zola ("the symbol of everything which trembles and cries, faceless, before the eternally closed door of the invisible"), or of Reinach, who saw in it the allegory of grief, to the rather unique interpretations like, for instance, Lesser's. He sees the figure as a Christian prisoner waiting to be thrown to the lions. Landsberger suggests the figure represents Justice mourning the death of Savonarola. Most scholars recognize it as a rendering of biblical or classical themes. Venturi proposed that the figure is the levite Ephraim's concubine, abused by Belial's sons, while Antoniewicz, citing Ovid (*Fasti*, II, 721–852), suggests Lucretia and Tarquin. Mesnil accepts the family tradition that the figure is Rea Silvia. Other biblical episodes are cited as well: Esther; the king Assuerus, etc. We might be dealing here with one of the two *cassoni* (marriage chests) which Filippino Lippi did for the Torrigiani family; he painted all the episodes about Esther except the *Derelitta*. Since those works could not be later, stylistically, than 1480, the *Derelitta* should date to the same period. Thus Gamba, and later Mesnil, date it 1476. Bettini accepts the idea that the painting was part of the *cassoni* decoration, but dates it 1481.

Piccoli offers a highly allegorical interpretation: the figure in the Botticelli painting is Truth Abandoned, as related to a Mantegna-like print showing Ignorance laying siege to the house of Truth, along with Envy and Suspicion, while Virtue, blind and naked, is led by the hand by Error, followed by Trickery, to the tune played by Pleasure. Argan put more Neo-Platonic emphasis on the interpretation, claiming that here Virtue is separated from Knowledge, or Truth, in the sense of divine revelation.

Whatever the interpretation, the link with the *cassoni*, is highly improbable, despite the similarity in size, because the *Derelitta* or *Outcast* has too many definite stylistic features which associate it with the drawings from Dante and the *Calumny* (plates 92–93), bringing the date closer to 1495 as Venturi had already said. Other dates: Bode says a little before 1490; Yashiro, around 1483; and Argan, around 1490.

Plate 90

NUDE YOUTH. *Drawing, 16·9 × 10·5. Hamburg, Kunsthalle.* Published by A. Venturi as a study for the *Derelitta*, the drawing is accepted as autograph, dated near the Pallavicini panel (color plate III), by Pauli, Popham and Berenson. Even apart from the thematic similarity Venturi noted, the style obviously approaches the *Derelitta*. Since the drawing also shows relationships with the Dante drawings, a late date seems confirmed, for the *Derelitta* as well.

Plate 91

FAITH. *Drawing, 25 × 16·3. London, British Museum.* Pen on black pencil sketch. Robinson attributed it to Botticelli as early as 1876, but Horne, Berenson and Van Marle consider it a school product. On the other hand, some critics, like Gamba, Bettini, Popham and Pouncey, and Bertini, consider it autograph and propose 1495 as a date.

Plates 92–93

CALUMNY. *Panel, 62 × 91. Florence, Uffizi.* Transferred to the Uffizi from the Pitti Palace in 1773, it was described as an "allegorical story with small figures in the manner of Ghirlandaio." But it is unquestionably identifiable with the panel Vasari mentions as being in the house of Fabio Segni "inside, the *Calumny* by Apelles; where Sandro divinely imitated the caprice of that ancient painter, and gave it to Antonio Segni, his very dear friend." Antonio Segni was born in 1460; his son Fabio, in 1502. Since 1434, Alberti, in his *De Pictura*, had suggested to artists that they reproduce Apelles' *Calumny*, which had been described in Lucian's *De calumnia*. According to the research by R. Förster (1887), the earliest rendering of Apelles' *Calumny* is in the MS of Lucian translated by

Bartolomeo Fontio, which was produced in 1472 for Ercole I d'Este. Then there is Mantegna's drawing (or his school's), engraved by Girolamo Mocetto (now in the British Museum), and also a panel, now lost, "with the story of Calumny," recorded in the inventory taken at Lorenzo the Magnificent's death, in 1492. Botticelli derived the idea not only from Alberti's brief description, but from Lucian himself in Latin translations, by Guarino Veronese, done at the beginning of the fifteenth century, or by Bartolomeo Fontio, 1472, or the one printed in Florence in 1496. Alberti's description of the original *Calumny* runs: "The picture had a man with very large ears (Midas), next to whom on each side were two women; one was called Ignorance and the other, Suspicion. Further on, there was Calumny. She seemed at first sight quite beautiful, but her face was very astute and she carried in her right hand a lighted torch. With her left hand, she dragged a small boy along by the hair, and he was stretching his hands toward heaven. And there was a pale, ugly, filthy man, with an evil face, whom you might compare to someone who had lived by violence and was lean and fiery. He was Calumny's guide, and his name was Hate. And there were two other women, Calumny's companions, who arranged her dress and jewels. One was called Deceit and the other, Fraud. Behind them stood Penitence, dressed in mourning robes, which she herself continually tore. Lastly followed a young girl, bashful and modest, named Truth." Other details in Lucian's text are faithfully reproduced by Botticelli: the man on the throne extends his hand toward Calumny, Penitence turns to look at Truth.

As to figurative sources, Mid-deldorf (1958) has called attention to the derivation of the naked Truth from the two figures in bronze by Ghiberti on the doorposts of Andrea Pisano's doors in the Baptistery.

The mock statues and bas-reliefs adorning the hall the scene takes place in, are taken from the Bible, from mythology, from legends. Some are readily identifiable, for instance, the central scene on the base of the throne reproduces Zeusis' *Family of the Centaur*, described by Lucian (plate 98). The next two reliefs on the right show *Jove and Antiope*, and *Minerva with the Gorgon* (plate 98). The first statue on the right is *Judith*, and the mock reliefs above and below represent the murder of Holofernes and the return to Bethulia. The statue on the central pilaster, posed as Andrea del Castagno's Pippo Spano may be St George (Horne), who can be seen at the center of the vault killing the dragon. More likely the statue is Mars (Gamba) since he is placed under a relief where *putti* play with a lion. The next statue on the left (plate 97) may be David (Horne), because underneath, only partially visible, is a relief showing the nude David on Goliath's body. Gamba thinks the figure is Theseus, since above, he claims, we can see the scene of Bacchus finding the abandoned Ariane (plate 96b). But this might be better interpreted as Mars and Venus (Horne). The frieze beneath the vault at the extreme left might show Hercules pursuing Diomedes' horses (Horne). More clearly identifiable, on the upper base at the extreme left, we see Hercules and Lica, and Apollo and Daphne. On the base immediately to the right of Penitence, Horne sees the judg-ment of Paris. On the central vault,

next to the scene of St George killing the dragon, we can make out two scenes from the story of Mucius Scaevola (Horne). The central panel on the right vault may show the fall of the Titans. On the frieze on the right, we have a scene that is rather difficult to interpret: a woman leads a centaur with an *amorino* astride him, and the myth of Prometheus, followed by another scene where a wayfarer approaches a woman. At the extreme right of the base, there is the scene of the Justice of Trajan, and on the vault at the extreme left there are the three scenes from the story of Nastagio degli Onesti. Although a number of the scenes allude to the dispensation of justice, many others are rather heterogeneous and there-fore we cannot specify any unifying theme.

Critics agree that this is a late work, ranging from 1485–90, 1490–91 and 1494–95 (Horne, A. and L. Venturi, Gamba, Bettini, Mesnil and Argan). The style is distinct, on the one hand, from the *Coronation* done in 1490 (plate 42), and, on the other, from the *Mystic Nativity* done in 1501 (plate 114), and therefore the most probable date is the one most cited, that is, halfway between these works. We may want to give greater em-phasis to the importance of the publication of Lucian's works in 1496. Or we could accept Lands-berger's explanation that the painting symbolizes the scandal-mongering which led Savonarola to his death (1498 or later, which would be too late), if the scene alluded to the friar's excommunication in May, 1497.

Plate 94

CALUMNY. Detail: Calumny, with Deceit, Fraud and the victim.

Plate 95

CALUMNY. Detail: Midas, Ignorance and Suspicion.

Plate 96a

CALUMNY. Detail of the mock reliefs at the upper right: a woman leads a centaur ridden by an *amorino*, the myth of Prometheus, the wayfarer who approaches a woman.

Plate 96b

CALUMNY. Detail of the mock bas-reliefs at the upper left; Bacchus finds Ariane, or perhaps Venus and Mars.

Plate 97

CALUMNY. Detail of the left pilaster with the mock statue of Theseus, or David, and another under the arch.

Plate 98

CALUMNY. Detail of the mock reliefs on the base of the throne: the family of the centaur, Jove and Antiope, Minerva with the Gorgon.

Plate 99

THE FAITHLESS AND THE DESCENT OF THE HOLY GHOST. *Drawing. Darmstadt, Kupferstich-kabinett.* Identified as early as 1896 as a Botticelli by Schönbrunner and Meder, it was published by A. Venturi (1926) as a study made during the artist's stay in Rome. Berenson considered it a school product, but Van Marle, Gamba, Bertini and Argan think it autograph. They all date it the last decade of the century, around the time of the *Derelitta* (Plate 89) and the *Calumny* (plates 92–93). According to Argan's justifiable surmise, the subject is related to the *Derelitta* itself.

Plate 100

ANNUNCIATION. *Panel, 36 × 35. Hanover, Niedersächsische Landes-galerie.* Recognized and published by A. Venturi as a late work, close in time to the *Calumny* (plates 92–93) and to the *Derelitta* (plate 89), the painting is accepted by Van Marle (dating it 1490 c.); Berenson (dating it among the late works); Gamba (considering it a late improvisation); Mesnil (attributing the hasty workmanship to the *bottega*); Argan (considering it, again, a late work, conceived as far as the presence of the praying woman, as the "miraculous incarnation of the holy Mystery in the prayers of the devoted"). Other critics are non-committal. For the immediacy of expression alone, it merits being considered as autograph. Later than the *Annunciation* in the predella of the *Coronation* in the Uffizi (plate 47a), probably done around 1498.

Color Plate III

CALUMNY. Detail of plates 92–93.

Plate 101

JUDITH. *Panel, 36 × 37. Amsterdam, Von Rath Collection.* Richard von Kaufmann of Berlin acquired it from the London restorer, Buttery, around 1900. In 1914, it went to the König Collection in Amsterdam, and around 1930, to its present location. Published for the first time by Frizzoni (1902), who judged it later than the *Judith* in the Uffizi (cf. Part I, plate 44), the attribution is universally accepted.

It has been variously dated from 1490 to 1495. The line is harsher than in the *Calumny* (even if we compare it to the mock relief of *Judith*) and induces us to choose the later date, even 1497–1500. Gamba thinks it may have been part of the *Tragedies of Virginia* and of *Lucretia*, which can be dated around 1499 (plates 102–103).

Plate 102

TRAGEDY OF VIRGINIA. *Panel, 86 × 165. Bergamo, Accademia Carrara.* Morelli bought it at the Monte di Pietà (official pawn bank) in Rome and exhibited it at the Baths of Diocletian (Christian Exposition) in 1870, with an attribution to Botticelli. The Accademia acquired it as part of the Morelli bequest. The theme deals with Marcus Claudius's rape of Virginia, Appius Claudius's iniquitous decision (background), Virginia's murder of her daughter and her departure, and her instigation of the army to revolt (center foreground). The analogous panel in Boston (cf. comment on plate 103) derives from Livy and Valerius Maximus. Morelli assumed it was part of the series Vasari mentions as being in the Vespucci house, and Ulmann extended the possibility even to the Boston panel. Horne later discovered that the house in Via de' Servi mentioned by Vasari was not acquired by Giovanni Vespucci, but by his father Guidantonio on March 5, 1499. Thus it is probable the paintings were executed shortly after, and this is the date most frequently mentioned by the critics. But some scholars propose other dates: 1492, Bode; 1490–1500, Ulmann; 1490 c., Schubring; 1497–1500, Van Marle (probable); cf. also Berenson, in *Gazette des Beaux-Arts*, 1896; F. J. Mather and W. Rankin, in *The Burlington Magazine*, 1906. The Boston panel is sometimes considered inferior in quality to the Bergamo panel (Horne, Mesnil, etc.). Both panels in any case can be considered substantially autograph.

Plate 103

TRAGEDY OF LUCRETIA. *Panel, 80 × 178. Boston, Isabella Stewart Gardner Museum.* This belonged to the Ashburnham Collection (England) and was exhibited as a Botticelli at a showing of Italian primitives at the New Gallery in London in 1893–94. Shortly after, it was acquired by Mrs. Gardner. The painting shows Lucrece attempting to resist Tarquin. At the right, Lucretia commits suicide, and in the center, before her corpse, Brutus incites the people to revolt. (For derivation, chronology, etc., cf. comment on plate 102.)

Plate 104

TRAGEDY OF VIRGINIA. Detail: the left side, the rape of Virginia.

Plate 105

TRAGEDY OF VIRGINIA. Detail: the right side, the murder and Virginia's departure for the camp.

Plate 106

TRAGEDY OF VIRGINIA. Detail: the right side, the chiaroscuro over the door.

Plate 107

TRAGEDY OF LUCRETIA. Detail of the center: the people revolt at the sight of Lucretia's body.

Plate 108

TRAGEDY OF LUCRETIA. Detail: the right side, Tarquin's violence.

Color Plate IV

MYSTIC NATIVITY. Detail of plate 114.

Plate 109

TRAGEDY OF LUCRETIA. Detail: the left side, Lucretia commits suicide.

Plate 110

TRAGEDY OF LUCRETIA. Detail of the center: mock statue of Judith and mock reliefs above.

Plate 111

MIRACLE OF ST JOHN EVANGELIST. *Drawing, 29·5 × 23. Paris, Louvre.* Pen on silk. Judged a school derivation by Berenson, it is none the less considered autograph by Yashiro (who refers it to about 1491) and by Gamba (who more correctly places it around the end of the century).

Plate 112

AGONY IN THE GARDEN. *Panel, 53 × 35. Granada, Capilla de los Reyes.* Published by Gomez Moreno (1908) among the works of art in the royal chapel Isabella the Catholic had built just before her death (1504) near the mosque. Charles V later transformed the mosque to a cathedral, and decorated it with works of art from the chapel. In a note to Gomez Moreno's article, Bertaux attributed the panel to the school, but Yashiro considered it autograph. Van Marle, Berenson, Gamba, Mesnil, Bettini and Argan agree; they all tend to place it just before 1504. But we cannot claim that the panel was painted expressly for the chapel, and indeed, it may have already been in the queen's collection. The style seems to fit in with the *Tragedies of Virginia and Lucretia* (plates 102–103) which date around 1499, rather than with the *Mystic Nativity* in London (plate 114), painted around 1501. Therefore, it seems more appropriate to accept Van Marle's hypothesis of a date just before 1500 than to accept the more widely cited date. A. Venturi and others pass over the painting in silence.

Plate 113

ANNUNCIATION. *Panel, 49·5 × 58·5. Glasgow, Art Gallery and Museum.* Originally in the McClellan Collection in Glasgow. Waagen recorded it as a Botticelli, and it is generally accepted to be autograph and placed around 1500 (cf. also R. Fry, in *The Burlington Magazine,* 1919). Berenson, Mesnil and A. Venturi have reservations. But the quality of the work leaves no question it is autograph, near in time to the *Tragedies of Virginia and Lucretia* (plates 102–103).

Plate 114

MYSTIC NATIVITY. *Canvas, 108·5 × 75. London, National Gallery.* Acquired from the Aldobrandini Villa in Rome probably around 1798–99 (perhaps it had come from the Aldobrandini family in Florence), it was noted in William Young Ottley's collection in 1811, and already known as a Botticelli. Ottley thought the painting was part of the altarpiece of Santa Maria Novella, which today, however, has been identified with the *Adoration* in the Uffizi (cf. Part I, plate 52). It was sold in 1837, and in 1851 became part of the Fuller Maitland Collection at Stansted Hall (Essex), from where it was taken to London in 1878. An epigraph in Greek at the top of the canvas contains not only the artist's name and date of execution, but also some obscure apocalyptic expressions (discussed fully by Horne, Mesnil, Davies and Pope-Hennessy ("Sandro Botticelli: The Nativity," *The Gallery Books,* 15, London n.d.). A literal translation would be: "I, Alessandro, painted this painting at the end of 1500 during the troubles in Italy, in the half time after the time, according to the eleventh chapter of St

John in the second grief of the Apocalypse, in the three-and-a-half-year liberation from the devil; after, he will be chained during the twelfth and we shall see him . . . (erasure: 'trod upon' or better 'precipitated') . . . just as in this painting." Since the Florentine year began on March 25, the term "end of 1500" would mean the first three months of 1501 in our calendar. The "troubles in Italy" could refer generally to the wars, the French invasions and the other difficulties which plagued the country and Florence after the death of Lorenzo the Magnificent (1492). Perhaps, more exactly, he is referring to the disastrous military enterprises of Cesare Borgia, Duke Valentino, who laid siege to Faenza in the early months of 1501 and threatened Tuscany. Florence was alarmed, and, in fact, in May, Borgia's troops were camped just a few miles away, at Campi Bisenzio. The second grief of chapter 11 of the Apocalypse prophesies the oppression of the holy city for forty-two months (three and a half years) while two witnesses dressed in sackcloth prophesy, devouring their enemies with the flames that come from their mouths, for 1,260 days (three and a half years) until the monster from the abyss (Antichrist) shall make war on them and kill them, and their bodies will lie unburied for three and a half days. Then they will arise and ascend into heaven. At that moment an earthquake will destroy the tenth part of the city and seven thousand men, while the others will glorify God and voices from heaven will announce the kingdom of the Lord. Chapter 12 of the Apocalypse tells of the fall of Satan and the rebel angels from Heaven. Thus it would seem legitimate to interpret the painting as derived from the sermons of

Savonarola or from the events of his "mission": the two martyred witnesses would be the Friar himself and Fra Domenico da Pescia (Silvestro Maruffi was of secondary importance); the sacks they dressed in, their robes; flames from their mouths, their sermons (and in fact Savonarola interpreted this passage from the Apocalypse in a commentary to the Vulgate which he possessed).

The painting generally follows the Gospel according to St Luke and interprets the Nativity as the triumph of God's kingdom. Thus it is a prophecy of the liberation from grief yet to come and of the peace which will reign among men after the Antichrist, marked by the condemnation of Savonarola and the "troubles in Italy." The major difficulty with this interpretation is precisely the phrase of the epitaph: ". . . in the half time after the time" from Apocalypse 12:4, which apparently Savonarola in his gloss interpreted as "a year and two years and the half of a year." The time indicated would be about a year and a half, but if this were so, it would not coincide with Savonarola's execution (May 25, 1498), but only with Duke Valentino's attack. Since we are not certain about Botticelli's own interpretation, calculations become extremely complex. In any case, to support the interpretation from Savonarola, Pope-Hennessy observes that the Nativity is here rendered in a way that recalls Savonarola's Christmas sermons for 1493 and 1494, when the Friar asked those who wanted Florence to become the new Nazareth to go spiritually to the Manger, where they would find Mary adoring the Infant, along with three maidens (Grace, Truth and Justice). In the painting they may be seen as the three angels over the manger.

The epigraph, furthermore, with its promise of suffering and renewal, is very much related to the spirit of Savonarola's prophecies.

We would add, however, that the three men the angels are embracing are not Savonarola and his fellow martyrs.

Plate 115

MYSTIC NATIVITY. Detail of the Manger.

Plates 116–117

MYSTIC NATIVITY. Detail: the epigraph, the angelic choir and the angels over the Manger.

Plate 118

MYSTIC NATIVITY. Detail: the center pair of angel and man embracing.

Plate 119

MYSTIC CRUCIFIXION. *Canvas, 73 × 51. Cambridge, Massachusetts, Fogg Art Museum.* It was acquired in Florence around 1900, and belonged to the Aynard Collection in Lyons. Very damaged and partly repainted, it was cleaned in 1929, but still appears quite worn. Horne published it for the first time (1908) as a work of Botticelli partly done by the school and dated it close to the *Mystic Nativity* in London (plate 114). His opinion has been accepted, and the work recognized as a late masterpiece, done after 1500. But any allegorical interpretation falls short of a complete explanation. Horne related the painting to Savonarola's vision of *Crux irae Dei* (the Cross of God's Wrath) in his *Compendium of Revelations*; that is, that God's anger falls upon Florence for her sins. Mary Magdalene, who lies at the foot of the Cross, represents repentant humanity, while the angel at the right beating the fox is symbolically punishing vice (the fox and the grapevine from the Song of Solomon 2:15). Bode saw the fox as a lion, however, and interpreted it as the *Marzocco* or heraldic symbol of Florence, and Mary Magdalene as repentant Florence. Gamba reads the allegory more positively: God is protecting Florence from the punishments that are inflicted on the world, and the beating of the animal (fox) means the triumph of religion over the licentiousness of humanism.

While there are other variants on this basic interpretation, the allegory becomes clearer if we consider the painting as freely inspired from Savonarola's sermon, "For the Renewal of the Church," which he gave on January 13, 1495: "I saw in my imagination a black cross over Babylon Rome, and there was written on it *"Ira Domini"* and on it rained swords, knives, lances and all the arms, hail and stones with great and awful thunder and lightning and the air was very dark and black. And I saw another cross, in gold, which came from the sky over Jerusalem, and on it was written *"Misericordia Dei"* and there the air was serene and clear. By this vision, I tell you that God's Church must be renewed and soon, because God is angry . . ."

The painter combines the two crosses into one, with Christ, in a golden yellow, which truly comes from the sky to earth. At Christ's left, the stormy clouds from which the demons hurl fiery swords on the earth. At the right of the Cross, Florence lies in the sun and God sends white angels (almost invisible because of the damage), who bear shields crossed in red, inspired from another vision in the same sermon: "I saw a sword over Italy and it trembled, and I saw angels who came and had red crosses in their hands . . ."

It seems clear to me, therefore, to understand this painting as an allegory of purification of Florence and of the Church, which are both repentant after the punishments symbolized by the clouds God's angels are forcing from the city, while the beast of vice is punished and the wolf of corruption is driven from the Church. The renewal of the Church and the purification of Florence, the New Jerusalem, are closely united in Savonarola's thought. If we interpret the painting in this way, we see how close it is to the *Mystic Nativity* in London. Certainly it is substantially autograph and stylistically related to the *Nativity*. And it may have been painted, as Gamba suggests, when the threat posed by Duke Valentino was overcome in 1501–02.

Plate 120

VOCATION OF ST ZENOBIUS. *Panel, 66·5 × 149·5. London, National Gallery.* From the left: St Zenobius gives up marriage and receives baptism from the bishop, Theodosius. Then follows the baptism of Sophia, Zenobius's mother, in the presence of her husband and the saint. Pope Damasus consecrates Zenobius as bishop. This and the three paintings reproduced in plates 122, 124–125, formed a series of panels used as benchbacks; that is, panels which fitted into the wood paneling of a room, probably in one of the confraternities dedicated to the saint in Florence. The first to appear was the panel in Dresden (plate 125), published for the first time with Botticelli's name in the *Kunstblatt*, 1823 and 1824, and commented on by Rumohr. Without citing his sources, he claimed the panel came from the Company of St Zenobius (which is now doubtful; cf. Poggi, in *Rivista d'Arte*, 1916). In the first half of the nineteenth century, it was part of the Metzger Collection in Florence, and in 1868 it went to its present location from the Von Quandt Collection in Dresden. The two panels in London (this one and plate 122) became known in 1891 when the Mond Collection in London acquired them from Palazzo Rondinelli, in Via della Stufa in Florence. In 1894, they were put on exhibition as autograph paintings in the Burlington House show of that year. In 1924, they were transferred to the National Gallery, as part of the Mond bequest. The panel in New York (plate 124), formerly in Milan and then Berlin, has been recorded since 1911, when they were put on sale with the rest of the Abdy Collection in London. It was even then attributed to Botticelli, and Burroughs published it in 1911. After Ulmann judged it a late work, of around 1498–1500, recent criticism has generally agreed, with some variations in the dating. Richter and Bode prefer a date around 1495, while Horne, Gamba, Mesnil, Bettini and Argan prefer, more justifiably, a date around 1500–1505. Horne cites the hagiographic source as being the *Summa historialis* of St Anthony, printed in Basel in 1491.

Plate 121a

VOCATION OF ST ZENOBIUS. Detail of the left side: the saint renounces marriage and leaves his promised bride and his family.

Plate 121b

VOCATION OF ST ZENOBIUS. Detail from the center: Bishop Theodosius baptizes the saint.

Plate 122

MIRACLES OF ST ZENOBIUS. *Panel, 65 × 139·5. London, National Gallery.* From the left: St Zenobius frees two youths who had mistreated their mother from her curse; revives the son of a noblewoman of France, who had been entrusted to him while she went on a pilgrimage to Rome and had died in his mother's absence; cures a blind man who promised to become a Christian if he regained his sight. (Cf. also comment on plate 120.)

Plate 123a

MIRACLES OF ST ZENOBIUS. Detail of the left side: the saint frees two youths from their mother's curse.

Plate 123b

MIRACLES OF ST ZENOBIUS. Detail of the center: the saint revives the dead boy.

Plate 124

MIRACLES OF ST ZENOBIUS. *Panel, 68 × 151. New York, Metropolitan Museum.* At the right in the background, St Zenobius heals a sick person in a convent; in the foreground, at the left, he revives a dead man; he heals a man fallen from a horse. Then the deacon Eugenius heals a woman or brings her back to life. The panel had been considerably altered by repainting in the central section. (Cf. also the comment on plate 120.)

Plate 125

MIRACLES OF ST ZENOBIUS. *Panel, 69 × 139·6. Dresden, Gemäldegalerie.* From the left: a cart crushes a boy; the deacon Eugenius picks him up; St Zenobius brings him back to life, and Eugenius gives him back to his mother. The saint announces to the faithful that his death is imminent.

Plate 126

MIRACLES OF ST ZENOBIUS. *(Dresden.)* Detail from the center: the saint brings a dead boy back to life.

LOST PAINTINGS

PANEL OF THE HIGH ALTAR. *Florence, Church of San Pier Gattolini.* Recorded by the *Anonimo Gaddiano* without a description of the subject. The church was destroyed when Cosimo I had new fortifications built.

DRINKING BACCHUS. *Florence, Medici Wardrobe.* Vasari records a "Bacchus puts a basin to his mouth" in the "wardrobe of Duke Cosimo." This must be the same as the "portrait of Bacchus on canvas three arms high" which we find in the inventory of Cosimo I's personal possessions.

ST FRANCIS. *Florence, Monastery of Santa Maria di Monticelli.* This may have been a fresco, for which Botticelli was paid on June 14 and August 14, 1496.

FORTUNE. *Florence, Medici Palace.* The inventory taken on the death of Lorenzo the Magnificent registers a bedstead in Piero's antechamber, with a "cover to said bed in said antechamber painted with a Fortune by hand of Sandro Botticelli." (Cf. Müntz, *Les collections des Médicis au XVe siècle,* 1888.)

ASSUMPTION. *Pisa, Duomo, Chapel of the Incoronata.* Vasari records an unfinished fresco, which is also documented by payments made from July to September, 1474. It was to serve as a trial for an eventual commission for frescoes in the Pisa Cemetery. Destroyed in 1583.

PALLAS. *Florence, Medici Palace.* A standard included in the inventory made on the death of Lorenzo the Magnificent (1492). It was executed for the joust of 1475.

THE HANGED TRAITORS. *Florence, Old Bargello, next to the Palazzo Signoria (over the Customs Door).* Fresco of the condemned Pazzi conspirators painted in 1478 and destroyed in 1494.

FRESCOES. *Volterra, Spadaletto Villa.* Recorded very generally by Vasari and by Ludovico il Moro's agent in a letter dated a little after 1485.

CARTOONS FOR MOSAICS. *Florence, Duomo, Chapel of San Zanobi.* Work was begun in 1491 and interrupted.

DECORATIVE FRESCOES. *Florence, Villa in Castello.* Carried out in 1497.

PANEL FOR THE HIGH ALTAR. *Montevarchi, Church of St Francis.* Vasari cites it, but we have no other information.

BALDACHIN. *Florence, Orsanmichele.* Vasari says, ". . . and it was he (Botticelli) who was among the first to be given the task of preparing the standards and other draperies, as they say, by commission, so that the colors will not fade will show their colors on every band. And by his hand, the baldachin of Orsanmichele, full of Madonnas, all different and lovely." We have no other information.

EMBROIDERIES. *Florence, Church of Santa Maria Novella.* Vasari cites it: "Botticelli was generous with the figures in the stories, as can be seen from the embroideries of the frieze around the cross which the monks of Santa Maria Novella carry in procession, all his design."

MADONNA AND CHILD WITH ST JOHN THE BAPTIST AND AN ANGEL. *Florence, Trofei house.* Borghini records this panel (1584) in the Trofei family: "the Virgin, the Child on the ground, held by a lamb, next to whom is the young St John and a very beautiful landscape."

PORTRAIT OF SIMONETTA CATTANEO VESPUCCI or of FIORETTA GORINI. *Florence, Medici Palace.* Vasari says: "In the Grand Duke Cosimo's wardrobe, there are two very beautiful heads of women in profile by his (Botticelli's) hand, one of whom, they say, is the beloved of Giuliano de' Medici." Sometimes identified as the *Portrait of a Young Woman* in the Pitti Palace (cf. comment on plate 51, Part I).

PORTRAIT OF LUCREZIA TORNABUONI. *Florence, Medici Palace.* Vasari records two profiles of women and another of Lucrezia de' Tornabuoni, but he mistakenly identifies her as Lorenzo's wife, when she was in fact his mother. Lucrezia Tornabuoni's portrait is also recorded in an inventory of 1553, as Horne noted (cf. comment on plate 51, Part I).

ADORATION OF THE MAGI. *Florence, Palazzo Signoria.* A fresco listed among Botticelli's works by the *Anonimo Gaddiano*, described as being at the head of the stairs in front of the Door of the Catena. Disappeared when the interior was remodeled, before Vasari's time. For the attempts to identify it, cf. comments on plates 70 and 71.

ATTRIBUTED PAINTINGS

Plate 127

PORTRAIT OF A YOUNG WOMAN. *Panel, 82 × 54. Frankfurt, Städelsches Kunstinstitut.* Warburg believed it was the portrait of Simonetta Vespucci, and both he and Ulmann considered it autograph, dating it between 1480 and 1486. Ulmann doubted it was Simonetta because the figures of Apollo and Marsias on the pendant were Medici symbols, and therefore he would only go so far as to say the painting was executed for one of them. Among recent critics, only Van Marle continues to believe it is authentic because, he says, of its fine quality, and to believe the sitter is Simonetta. He bases his opinion on the portrait by Piero di Cosimo at Chantilly, the inscription on which he considers genuine. In fact, he believes this painting to be the source for the posthumous one at Chantilly, since, according to Van Marle, Simonetta was still alive when it was painted, not later than 1476. But Horne, Bode (who thought it a school product of about 1480, but then changed his mind and said it might be authentic and dateable around 1478) and A. Venturi reject the attribution. Gamba, Berenson, L. Venturi and Mesnil also disagree with Van Marle. Other writers do not cite it. Although of better quality than the one in Berlin (plate 128), it is none the less a workshop painting deriving from the *Venus and Mars* in London (plate 8). Related to the painting, and to the others of the same kind, is a drawing in the Ashmolean in Oxford, which Bertini published (1953).

Plate 128

PORTRAIT OF A YOUNG WOMAN. *Panel, 47·5 × 35. Berlin, Staatliche Museen.* Bode published it as probably authentic in 1888, claiming it was the portrait of Simonetta Vespucci. He repeated his opinion later because, he said, the portrait by Piero de Cosimo at Chantilly supported it. At first he dated it around 1480, then he judged it to be earlier, around 1476. Even Schmarsow considered it authentic, and dated it around the Roman period, close to the *Lady* in Altenburg (cf. Part I, plate 37). Van Marle thinks it authentic but doubts that the sitter is Simonetta because of the differences from the Frankfurt portrait (plate 127) and proposes that it is the portrait of Lucrezia Tornabuoni Vasari mentions in Cosimo I's possession. He points out the similarities between this face and the face in Ghirlandaio's *Visitation* in Santa Maria Novella. Ulmann, Horne, A. Venturi, Berenson, Gamba, L. Venturi and Mesnil think it a workshop painting. Others are noncommittal. Too hard and stiff to be Botticelli's, the painting is undoubtedly one of the series of ideal women painted by the workshop after 1480. Inferior in quality to the portrait in Frankfurt (plate 127), also a workshop product.

Plate 129a

PORTRAIT OF A YOUNG WOMAN. *Panel, 63 × 44. Formerly in Munich, Bernheim Antiquarian.* It once belonged to the Seymour Collection in London and the Kappel in Berlin. In

1939, it was reported at Bernheim's, the antiques dealer. In 1893, it had appeared in a London show attributed to Botticelli and identified as the portrait of Simonetta Vespucci, along with the two small paintings in Berlin and formerly in Richmond (plates 126, 129b). Yashiro, Bode, Schmarsow, L. Venturi consider it authentic, but other writers are non-committal. Horne and A. Venturi reject it as an early copy, Van Marle considers it inferior to the Frankfurt version. Gamba does not think it genuine either, while Mesmil is silent. It is certainly the best among this group, and we detect that lively sense of line which marks the master's work. I would date it around 1480, at the time of *Venus and Mars* in London (plate 8).

Plate 129b

PORTRAIT OF A YOUNG WOMAN. *Canvas, 58 × 40. Formerly in Richmond, Cook Collection.* It was considered Botticelli's and identified as Simonetta while in the Stirling Collection in London. Cavalcaselle accepted the attribution but doubted the identification. Crowe considered it superior to the Berlin version (plate 128) and thought the sitter Lucrezia Tornabuoni. Recent criticism, for the most part, has tended to ascribe it to the *bottega*, and to deny the identification with Simonetta Vespucci, made, generally, on the basis of Piero di Cosimo's famous *Cleopatra* in Chantilly. (Cf. comment on plate 51, Part I.) We are dealing here with a copy, probably executed outside the *bottega*, which can be related to the similar portraits in Berlin and Frankfurt, and to the *Mars and Venus* in London.

Plate 130

PORTRAIT OF A YOUNG WOMAN.

and on the reverse, AN ANGEL. *Panel, 59 × 40. London, National Gallery.* Formerly in the Barker Collection in London, it was put on exhibition in Leeds in 1868 as a portrait of Botticelli's wife [*sic*]. In 1874, it went to the Samuel Collection and was then held by the Misses Cohen. In 1906, it was given to the National Gallery as part of the Samuel bequest. Spielman considered it by the school, or perhaps by "Sandro's friend," but Kroeber thought the *recto* was by the artist and the *verso* by the school. Most of the critics are noncommittal, while Davies considers the artist a "pedestrian follower of Botticelli's." It derives from the version formerly in the Noak Collection in Berlin (plate 129a). A work characterized by a general "Botticellianism" it reminds us of Botticini or of his circle. The meaning of the figure on the reverse is obscure.

Plate 131a

VENUS. *Canvas, 157 × 68. Berlin, Staatliche Museen.* The *Book* of Antonio Billi, followed by Vasari, records several nude figures of women by Botticelli in the houses of Florentine citizens. Bode thought this *Venus* might be one of them, and indeed judged it a study from an ancient statue of Venus for the *Birth of Venus* (plates 12–13). Schmarsow agreed with Bode, but he preferred thinking it was a portrait of Simonetta. Others (Ulmann) simply think it a copy by the artist. The opinion widely held from Morelli to Mesnil seems the most likely; that is, that the workshop did the copy for an admirer of the master's art.

Plate 131b

VENUS. *Canvas, 148 × 62. Formerly in Lucerne, private collection.* It was acquired in Florence from the Palazzo Feroni in 1850 and was in the Davenport Bromley Collection until 1863, when it went to the Ashburton in Bath House. It survived the fire there (although Horne thought it had been destroyed) and was put on the antiques market in 1920. It was recorded at Bohler's in Munich and later in Lucerne. Waagen ascribed it to the artist but Cavalcaselle to the workshop. A.Venturi published it as authentic, but it is generally regarded as by the workshop or an imitator.

Plate 132

VENUS. *Panel, 174 × 77. Turin, Galleria Sabauda.* It was acquired in Florence in 1844 and was in the Davenport Bromley Collection in London until 1863, when it went to the Ashburton at Bath House. The painting survived the fire there (Horne thought it destroyed) and after 1920 was acquired by the Gualino Collection, where it remained until 1930. The Italian Embassy in London had it until 1940, when the outbreak of the war forced its removal to its present location. Waagen regarded it as authentic, but Cavalcaselle considered it a workshop product. A. Venturi published it as authentic in 1925 and L. Venturi in 1926, followed by Van Marle. Generally regarded as by the workshop, the painting nonetheless has a liveliness in the line and a freshness of invention (although mannered) which might be compared to the rendering of the *Birth of Venus*, and suggests Botticelli was partly involved in its execution.

Plate 133a

MADONNA AND CHILD. *Panel. Formerly in Berlin, Simon Collection.* It once belonged to James Mann in Scotland. Cook published it as a probable Botticelli, and both A. Venturi and the writers of the catalog for the Simon sale considered it an extremely faithful and autograph copy of the *Madonna* in the altarpiece in Berlin (plate 20). More rightly considered a workshop copy—even though it is of high quality—by Van Marle and Gamba.

Plate 133b

MADONNA AND CHILD, ST JOHN THE BAPTIST AND AN ANGEL. *Round panel, diameter 86.5. Cincinnati, Edwards Collection.* It went from the Salting Collection in London to the Benson Collection in 1885. Fiocco published it as authentic in 1930, and dated it in relation to the *Madonna of the Pomegranate* (plate 25), that is, around 1487. It seems a workshop painting, although of good quality, executed after the master's drawing.

Plate 134a

JESUS AND ST JOHN THE BAPTIST. *Panel, 37.5 × 25.5. Ottawa, National Gallery of Canada.* It came from Böhler's, the antique dealers, in Lucerne in 1927. A. Venturi published it as an autograph painting of about the time of the *Madonna of the Magnificat* (plate 1), and Bode accepted it in the Botticelli oeuvre, dating it around 1485-90. Yashiro accepted it (dating it around 1487), and the catalog of the Italian Exhibition in London (1930), Van Marle and the catalog of the Canadian National Gallery carry it as authentic. On the other hand, Berenson, Gamba, and L. Collobi Ragghianti, who thinks it a fragment of a *Venus and Amorini*, regard it as a workshop product. A work, we would say, from the *bottega*, probably done around 1487-90.

Plate 134b

PORTRAIT OF A YOUTH. *Panel 57 × 38. Paris, Louvre.* It was successively in the Frizzoni Salis, Hainauer (Berlin) and Schlichting (Paris) collections. The attribution to Botticelli was made by Bode, followed by F. Harck, Ulmann, A. Venturi and with some reservations by Van Marle, who dated it prematurely at about 1474. Later Bode withdrew the attribution, and Venturi reconsidered, and downgraded it to a school effort following the opinion of Trubnikov (*Starye Godye*, April 1911). Kroeber denied it was a Botticelli because of the Flemish influences in it, and related it to Ghirlandaio. The portrait is still shown as a Ghirlandaio in the Louvre, and catalogued as such by Berenson. L. Collobi Ragghianti renewed the attribution to Botticelli, dating it to 1485. There are retouchings and overpainting, which have sentimentalized the Botticelli forms. But there is also a certain rigidity in the direction of Ghirlandaio. The painting cannot really be attributed to either artist.

Plate 135

MADONNA OF THE CANDLES. *Round panel, diameter 192. Formerly in Berlin, Kaiser Friedrich Museum.* Lost during the Second World War. Morelli confirmed the traditional attribution to Botticelli (*Die Galerie an Berlin*, 1893) and insisted it was authentic, while J. Meyer (in *Jahrbuch der preussischen Kunstsammlungen*, 1890) and Frizzoni argued that the workshop had collaborated. Later critics agree that the work is by a follower, except Bode, who finds that the painting was executed in large measure by the master himself. In fact, Ulmann and others thought it should be identified with the

tondo painted in Botticelli's *bottega* by his follower Biagio for the Church of San Francesco (San Salvatore al Monte) and object of one of Vasari's jokes. But Biagio di Antonio Tucci, who we know was Sandro's assistant, was born in 1446, while the *tondo* reflects the later style of the master and cannot be dated earlier than 1490, when Biagio was in his forties. Furthermore, Vasari's little story describes the *tondo* as having eight angels, and not seven (cf. comment on plate 63, Part I). The perspective structure was studied by J. Kern (1905).

Plate 136

ANNUNCIATION. *Panel, 106 × 113. Formerly in Berlin, Kaiser Friedrich Museum.* Lost during the war. Although Cavalcaselle regarded it as authentic, it is generally held to be a mediocre workshop copy of the *Annunciation* in the Uffizi (plate 38). It is difficult to agree with Mesnil that Botticelli did some of the painting.

Plate 137a

SPRING. *Panel, 78 × 21. New York, Knoedler Galleries.* Along with the panels reproduced in plates 137b–138b, it came from the Earl of Roseberg's collection in London. The four allegories were put on exhibition at the Royal Academy in London in 1878 by Hannah de Rothschild with Botticelli's name on them. Ulmann recorded them in 1893, but suspended judgment on the attribution. L. Venturi later published them as authentic and dated them about 1485–90. Important efforts in Botticelli's manner, but certainly by some hand other than the master's.

Plate 137b

SUMMER. *Panel, 78 × 21. New York, Knoedler Galleries.* Cf. comment on previous plate.

Plate 138a

AUTUMN. *Panel, 76 × 21·5. New York, Knoedler Galleries.* Cf. comment on plate 137a.

Plate 138b

WINTER. *Panel, 80 × 23. New York, Knoedler Galleries.* Cf. comment on plate 137a.

Plate 139

MADONNA AND CHILD, ST JOHN THE BAPTIST AND AN ANGEL. *Round panel, diameter 84·5. London, National Gallery.* Toward the end of the eighteenth century, it belonged to Abbot Carlo Bianconi (d. 1802) of Bologna and Milan, and was acquired by the Gallery from his heir, Giovanni Giuseppe Bianconi, in 1855. At first attributed to Ghirlandaio (P. Bassani, *Guida agli amatori delle B. A. . . . per la città di Bologna,* 1816), it was then ascribed to Botticelli in the *Catalog of the Paintings and Sculpture Owned by the Bianconi Family,* 1854 (in Italian). The National Gallery then listed the painting as a Botticelli. Cavalcaselle deprecated its value, and from Ulmann on, it has been considered a workshop product. Van Marle ascribed it to his "first student" and dated it between 1482 and 1486, but Gamba's estimate seems more probable; that is, around 1490. On the reverse we can read "M. (Maestro?) Giuliano da San Ghallo," and Richter interpreted this to be the famous architect's work. Apart from the fact that the style does not at all resemble the few drawings by Sangallo we have, the fact that the writing is on the back and oblique, as Davies has pointed out, might indicate that it was a kind of memorandum to send the panel to Sangallo to frame. Records indicate he did this work for Ghirlandaio, that is the frame for the *Adoration of the Magi* in the church of the Ospedale degli Innocenti (1498), and for Botticelli himself—the frame for the altarpiece in Santo Spirito, now in Berlin (plate 20). However, for a thoroughly argued thesis that the writing does indicate the work is by Sangallo, see Degenhardt, 1955. The hypothesis that the writing indicated the owner (Mesnil, etc.) is less probable. The work is of good quality, and came from Botticelli's workshop around 1490.

Plate 140

NATIVITY. *Round panel, diameter 76. Boston, Isabella Stewart Gardner Museum.* This went from the Duke of Brindisi's collection (Florence) to the Gardner Museum about 1900. Ulmann and Gamba thought it authentic, while Horne and Berenson considered the whole painting a workshop product, and Van Marle and Mesnil only part. Everyone agrees in dating it around 1490. Horne's attribution to the same artist who did the *Madonna* formerly in the Heseltine collection and now in the Rockefeller (plate 141) is unacceptable because the *Madonna* is much closer to Botticelli's style. Although the *Nativity* is of high quality, the Signorelli elements (which Gamba noticed) preclude the attribution to Botticelli.

Plate 141

MADONNA AND CHILD WITH ST JOHN THE BAPTIST. *Panel, 46 × 37. New York, John D. Rockefeller Jr. Collection.* Once belonging to Charles Somerwell, it was acquired in 1884 by J. P. Heseltine of London, and was exhibited in 1894 at Burlington House with Botticelli's name. Ulmann regarded it as authentic and related it in time to the *Madonnas* in the Poldi-Pezzoli (plate 3) and to the

177

Madonna of the Magnificat (plate 1), that is, according to his chronology, around 1482. Yashiro, Van Marle, Berenson and Gamba also consider it genuine and all date it around the time of the *Madonna of the Pavilion* in the Ambrosiana (plate 54), that is, around 1491 or shortly after. An excellent work from the school, with some help from the master: so say Horne, Bode and Mesnil, even though they agree with the date. The painting is very fine, and certainly based on the master's cartoon. Botticelli must have participated in the painting of the Madonna and of the mythological frieze on the parapet.

Plate 142

MADONNA AND CHILD WITH ST JOHN. *Panel, 124 × 85. Boston, Museum of Fine Arts.* Once in the Bammeville Collection and then in the Barker Collection in London, where Waagen saw it in 1857. It came to its present location in 1895. After it was cleaned in 1930, Hendy published it as authentic and referred it to the period between 1480 and 1485. Yashiro considers it a school effort and, to be exact, a copy of the *tondo* formerly belonging to the Lanckoronski in Vienna. Van Marle and Berenson also consider it a school product.

Plate 143

MADONNA AND CHILD WITH TWO ANGELS. *Round panel, diameter 112. Vienna, Akademie der Künst.* A gift from the Prince of Lichtenstein in 1890. We are certain that it came originally from the Canigiani house in Florence. Ulmann attributed it to Botticelli, but Horne, Mesnil and Van Marle (who thinks it derives from the *Madonna of the Magnificat*) consider it a school product. A good

painting from the school, done around 1490.

Plate 144

MADONNA AND CHILD WITH ST JOHN AND ANGELS. *Round panel, diameter 170. Rome, Borghese Gallery.* The Borghese family owned the painting since the beginning of the eighteenth century with an attribution to Ghirlandaio which was still carried in the 1833 inventory. Cavalcaselle and later Ulmann attributed it to Botticelli, dating it to about 1490. Bode dated it earlier (1485–90). Recently critics like De Rinaldis and Della Pergola have called it authentic. But Morelli had already in 1874, termed it a school painting done on the master's cartoon. But Berenson and Horne (in the unpublished second part of the ms. of 1908) assign it to the school completely, and in fact Horne discerned the hand of the artist who did the *Pomona* in Chantilly. Muratoff (*Starye Godye*, May 1911) linked it with the Chigi *tondo* and the Metcheresky *tondo* in Moscow. Van Marle and Mesnil also ascribed it to the school, and Mesnil observed that St John resembles the boy brought back to life in Filippino Lippi's fresco in the Carmine. Berenson and Gamba decided it was done jointly by Botticelli and a follower. The effort certainly is of high caliber, and I would incline to say it was done around 1490 by the artist of the *Pomona*, on the cartoon and with the help of the master.

Plate 145a

MADONNA AND CHILD. *Panel, 83 × 65. London, National Gallery.* Formerly owned by Count Angiolo Galli Tassi of Florence and bestowed by him to Santa Maria Nuova in 1863, the painting was acquired by the

National Gallery at Baslini's, the antiques dealer in Milan, in 1867. Frizzoni considered it authentic, and so did Ulmann, but for the most part, it has been regarded as a work done by the *bottega*. It derives from the *Madonna* in Dresden (plate 52). There are variations in Milan, in the Crespi Collection (formerly in Vienna and in Vaduz, in the Prince of Lichtenstein's collection, formerly Ginori's), in Frankfurt, the Städelsches Kunstinstitut, in the museum in Lille and in a private collection in Oxford.

Plate 145b

MADONNA AND CHILD, *Panel. Rome, Colonna Gallery.* Van Marle regarded it as a school effort, but most critics are noncommittal about it. Gamba thinks it is authentic, even if of minor note. A delicate workshop product, perhaps close to the *tondo* (plate 54) in the Ambrosiana.

Plate 146a

MADONNA AND CHILD WITH ST JOHN THE BAPTIST. *Round panel, diameter 95. London, National Gallery.* It went from the Patrizi Collection in Rome to the Salting in London, and from there to its present location in 1910. Ulmann considered it autograph and done around 1490, but Van Marle, Mesnil and Davies more rightly refer it to the *bottega*. Davies cites two variants that were formerly in the Fuller Maitland and Fairfax Murray collections.

Plate 146b

MADONNA AND CHILD WITH ANGELS. *Round panel, diameter 147. Florence, Corsini Gallery.* It went to the Corsini from the Medici villa at Careggi in the seventeenth century, along with a *tondo* by Filippino and a third by an anonymous Florentine. It is heavily overpainted and Caval-caselle thus had reservations when he made his judgment. Morelli considered it a follower's work on the master's cartoon. Horne considered it a derivation from the *St Barnabas Altarpiece* (plate 29). Ulmann, Bode, A. Venturi, Van Marle, Gamba, Mesnil regard it as by the workshop. Certainly a good piece from the workshop, painted around the 1490s, close to 1495. Not dissimilar from the *tondo* in the Borghese Gallery (plate 144).

Plate 147

TRANSFIGURATION, WITH SS AMBROSE AND AUGUSTINE. *Panel, 28 × 28. Rome, Pallavicini Collection.* De Nicola attributed it to Botticelli (cf. Cavalcaselle, ed. Langton Douglas, 1911, and in *Revue de l'Art*, 1912) and dated it after 1490. A. Venturi, Yashiro, Van Marle, Gamba and Bettini accept the attribution and date the painting between 1495 and 1499–1500. Mesnil rejects it, because he considers it the work of an imitator who did a whole series of Botticellian drawings. The vigor of the drawing, however, comes through the hasty and inferior execution and indicates that the work came from the *bottega* and was conceived by Botticelli himself. The probable chronology lies between 1490 and 1495, close to the *Lamentations* in Munich (plate 65) and in Milan (plate 66).

Plate 148

PENTECOST. *Panel, 221 × 229. Greenville, South Carolina, Bob Jones University.* Formerly in the Cook Collection in Richmond. It was already known to Ulmann who regarded it as a workshop painting. A. Venturi agreed, as well as Van Marle, who thought it may have been done by Raffaellino del Garbo.

Bode had originally judged it by the *bottega*, but later included it in the catalog of autograph works. Mesnil agreed it had been done by the workshop, but on the master's cartoon. Bettini proposed that the master had started it, but the shop had finished it, and dated it around 1495–99. Certainly by the workshop, even if conceived by the master. Close in time to the *Lamentations* in Munich (plate 65) and in Milan (plate 66); that is, before 1495.

Plate 149

ST SEBASTIAN. *Panel. Vatican City, Vatican Museums.* This comes from storage in Castelgandolfo (1923). In poor condition, it was restored in 1924–25 by Piero de Prai. A. Venturi published it as authentic and related in time to the *Lamentations* in Munich (plate 65) and in Milan (plate 66), but Van Marle and Gamba consider it the work of an imitator, in the master's late style.

Plate 150

LAMENTATION. *Panel, 107 × 69.5. Brussels, Bautier Collection.* Formerly in the Bourgeois Collection in Cologne. Horne records it as a copy somewhat later than the panel in the Poldi-Pezzoli (plate 66), but Mesnil considers it genuine except for some parts by the workshop, and he thinks it earlier and more authentic than the other. Most scholars are noncommittal about it, while Van Marle mentions it as a copy. The variation in Mary Magdalene's drapery (here we see her with her shoulders barely covered) is not, as Mesnil thought, a touch of fresh naturalism, but rather the copyist's addition and stylistically unjustified.

Plate 151a

ENTHRONED MADONNA. *Pane irregularly cut into a tondo, 79 × 86.*

Washington, D.C., National Gallery of Art. A. Venturi published it at Duveen's as an authentic work, close in time to the *Madonna of the Pomegranate* (plate 25). Gamba accepted the judgment, but dated it after the *Calumny* (plates 92–93). Van Marle attributed it to a follower, but most of the critics are noncommittal. I would say a work by the school of good quality, perhaps by the same artist who did the *Madonna* formerly belonging to Trotti (plate 151b). The *tondo* form is the result of uneven cutting.

Plate 151b

MADONNA AND CHILD. *Panel, 86 × 60. Formerly in Paris, Trotti House.* From the castle in Trebbio, it was acquired by Spencer Stanhope of Florence. It was sold in 1922 at G. Rabit's in Paris with Botticelli's name (in *Belvedere*, 1922). The attribution was accepted by A. Venturi, with a late dating. Van Marle, on the other hand, assigned it to the school and dated the panel around 1490–95. Critics are generally silent about it. Probably by the same hand as the previous panel.

Plate 152a

ANNUNCIATE ANGEL. *Round panel, diameter 15. Formerly in Florence, Corsini Gallery.* Just as the *Annunciate Virgin*, also once belonging to the Corsini, this panel is a fragment of a predella or frame. Ulmann knew of both works and considered them autograph and later than 1490. A. Venturi republished them as following the drawings from the *Divine Comedy*; that is, the last years of the century. Yashiro accepted it, but with a much earlier date, around 1483–84. Berenson considered it a late work, while Gamba thought it a "late improvisation of Botticelli's" and Mesnil a workshop product done around 1490. The rest of the critics are noncommittal. Very perceptible workshop copy of the *Annunciation* in Hanover (plate 100).

Plate 152b

ANNUNCIATE VIRGIN. *Round panel, diameter 15. Formerly in Florence, Corsini Gallery.* Cf. comment on plate 152a.

Plate 153

FLIGHT INTO EGYPT. *Transferred to canvas, 130 × 95. Paris, Musée Jacquemart-André.* Ulmann referred to Bode's attribution to Botticelli, and Bode reconfirmed it in 1926, dating the painting to about 1490–94. Schmarsow accepted the attribution, but gave a date of 1500 and later. For the most part, it is regarded as a workshop product. Gamba detects the same hand which did the *Coronation* at the Quiete near Florence—a work generally held to be by a follower. Certainly by the *bottega*, done around 1495–1500, but the conception of the central motif, as Mesnil has noted, must be the master's.

Plate 154

REDEEMER. *Panel, 47 × 33. Bergamo, Accademia Carrara (Morelli).* Morelli first attributed it to Botticelli, followed by A. Venturi, who dated it around 1500, and Berenson. Ulmann, Horne, Gamba, Mesnil, Bettini claim it is by an imitator. Of good quality, but the accentuated pietism of the typology and late style of Botticelli indicates the work of an imitator, perhaps someone working right in the *bottega*.

Plate 155a

TONDO OF THE MADONNA AND CHILD WITH ST JOHN. *Round panel,*

diameter 80·5, New York, Duveen Collection. It belonged to the Bauer and Schaeffer collections in Frankfurt and to the Leyland at Woolton Hall near Liverpool. Presented several times as an authentic work (*Catalogue of the Royal Academy, Old Masters,* 1876; Algernon Graves, *A Century of Loan Exhibitions,* 1913; Swarzenski and Gatz, *Austellung von Meisterwerken alter Malerei aus Privatbesitz,* 1925–26), it has been confirmed by Berenson, Lanton Douglas and M. W. Brockwell as Botticelli's dating around 1500. Van Marle thinks it by a follower. Quite fine and probably, according to Mesnil, conceived by the master and executed by the workshop.

Plate 155b

BAPTISM OF CHRIST. *Panel. Formerly in Faenza, Guidi Collection.* It was put on sale with the rest of the Guidi family collection at Sangiorgi's in Rome in 1902, and called a Botticelli. A. Venturi considered it a late and very damaged work by the master. The attribution was forgotten, perhaps because the painting has not been seen since the sale, but Ragghianti mentioned it again in 1954. Gamba, however, had justifiably judged it a school product (1936).

Plate 156

MADONNA AND CHILD. *Panel, 37 × 39. New York, Duveen Collection.* It passed from the Sarty to the Vendeuvre to the Grasset collections in Paris. The first description of it we have appeared in the catalog of an exhibition of the Alsatian and Lorraine artists in the French capital in 1874, but the first critical recognition came from L. Venturi in 1932. Mesnil considers it a workshop product, while Langton Douglas refers to it as genuine. A good painting, conceived by the master and executed by the workshop in the 1490s.

Plate 157

ST JEROME. *Drawing, 24·5 × 12·5. Florence, Uffizi.* Silverpoint and white lead on prepared grey-rose paper. Horne, Berenson, Yashiro, Van Marle and Gamba accepted the attribution to Botticelli. Bettini excludes it from the catalog because of its quality. A certain hardness in the touch induces our doubts about its authenticity. In any case, it is from Botticelli's workshop toward the end of the fifteenth century.

Plate 158a

ANNUNCIATE ANGEL. *Panel transferred to canvas, 45 × 31. Formerly in Leningrad, Hermitage.* Along with the *Annunciate Virgin* (plate 158b) and *SS Dominic and Jerome*, it was in the Hermitage from 1921 to 1926, originally in the Stroganoff Collection in Petersburg. Harck first spoke of Botticelli in connection with the painting in 1896; Benois accepted the attribution and Lazareff elaborated it, dating the drawing and the painting around 1495-98. A. Venturi, Yashiro, Van Marle and Gamba confirmed his opinion, including the date. But L. Venturi and Mesnil referred to it as a school work. Of remarkable quality, it was certainly done in the *bottega*, perhaps on Botticelli's cartoon.

Plate 158b

ANNUNCIATE VIRGIN. *Formerly in Leningrad, Hermitage.* Cf. comment on plate 158a.

Plate 159

CORONATION OF THE VIRGIN, WITH FOUR ANGELS AND TWO WORSHIPPERS. *Embroidery on the hood of a cope, 47 × 47. Milan, Poldi-Pezzoli Museum.* Acquired before 1900 with the drawing for the embroidery attributed to Botticelli. The attribution was reinforced by the label on the frame. Sant'Ambrogio recognized the seal of Portugal in the heraldic symbol at the bottom of the hood. He then hazarded that Jacopo of Lusitania, the famous Portuguese cardinal who had died at the age of twenty-six in Florence while on his way to Germany as papal legate for Pius II, had given the cope as a gift. Since the cardinal died on August 27, 1459, Sant' Agostino argued the design for the embroidery could not have been Botticelli's. But the stylistic characteristics clearly point to his late manner, in the last decade of the century. In fact, critics agree, with the exception of Van Marle who ascribes the drawing to Baldovinetti, that Botticelli prepared the cartoon for the embroidery.

MADONNA AND CHILD. *Panel. Formerly in London, Benson Collection.* Once in the Panciatichi Ximenes Collection in Florence, it went to the Carmichael Collection and then to the Benson. Cust noted the possibility of its being a Botticelli (1907), and it is carried as such in the Benson catalog (1914). But Horne and Van Marle justly identify it as a workshop variation of the altarpiece in Berlin (plate 20).

MADONNA AND CHILD WITH ST JOSEPH. *Panel, 51 × 38. Formerly in Berlin, the Simon Collection.* Fragment of an *Adoration of the Magi*, and once in the Langton Douglas and Butler collections, it was put on sale with the Simon Collection (1929) and carried in the sale catalog as a Botticelli (Friedländer). Bode verified it, but only Van Marle accepted his judgment and dated it around 1490. Certainly of that period, but a school product.

MADONNA AND CHILD WITH ST JOHN THE BAPTIST. *Round panel. Formerly in Vienna, Lanckoronski Collection.* Acquired, around 1890, from the Leclanché Collection. Ulmann attributed it to Botticelli as a late work, but for the most part it is ignored. Van Marle nonetheless listed it among the school works.

MADONNA AND CHILD WITH ST JOHN. *Formerly in Paris, Dreyfus Collection.* Published as authentic in the *Gazette des Beaux-Arts* (1897), it was considered partially autograph by J. Guiffrey (1908) and Reinach (1906). Berenson and Van Marle considered it a *bottega* panel. A variation by the school rather than by the workshop of the motif of the Pitti *Madonna* (plate 63).

NOLI ME TANGERE. *Panel, Private collection.* Van Marle mentioned it as an authentic work done around the time of the *Calumny.* I have not even seen a photograph of it.

RESURRECTION. *Private collection.* Cf. comment to preceding work.

CHRIST CROWNED WITH THORNS. *Panel. Formerly in Paris, Lazzaroni Collection.* Mesnil published it among the works done by the shop on Botticelli's conception and claimed it could be dated the second half of 1492 or later. He based his argument on the fact that on March 31 of that year the relic of Longinus's lance was first shown in public. The sultan, Bajazet, had given it to Pope Innocent VIII.

SAVIOR. *Canvas, 57·15 × 34·94. Cambridge, Massachusetts, Fogg Art Museum.* Van Marle published it as authentic (1928, 1931) and dated it around 1495. Most critics are noncommittal. Mesnil thinks it is an imitator's work, different from the painter who did the *Savior* in Bergamo (plate 154) and perhaps influenced by Northern painting. To be dismissed in any case, for reasons other than simply the differences with the Bergamo version.

THE YOUNG REDEEMER. *Panel. Formerly in New York, Kleinberger Galleries.* Published as authentic in the catalog of the exhibition of primitives at the Kleinberger Galleries (1929) and in *International Studio* (1929), it was accepted by Van Marle, who places it in the Roman period, close to the *Redeemer* in Detroit (Part 2, plate 106). It appears to be a school product, and the pietism is sufficient to date it later.

MADONNA AND CHILD WITH FOUR SAINTS. *Panel, 176 × 163 (predella: 14·5 × 98). Montelupo, Parish Church of San Giovanni.* Mesnil published it as authentic, but he later agreed with most critics that it is by the school, and dated it late in the century. Gamba detects some collaboration by Botticelli.

SS DOMINIC AND JEROME. *Panel transferred to canvas, 45 × 26. Formerly in Leningrad, Hermitage.* Part of the group with *Annunciate Angel* and the *Annunciate Virgin* (plates 158a–b) and involved in the same events. The quality is inferior, and there is no question that Botticelli did not contribute to its execution.

PORTRAIT OF A GENTLEMAN. *Panel. Rome, Lazzaroni Collection.* A. Venturi (1925) published it as authentic, but all the other critics are silent about it. The linear sensitivity and the image itself explain the attribution, but nonetheless the work is stylistically far from Botticelli's. Further, if it were his, the portrait could not be later than 1480, but the costume is sixteenth century. I think the painting could be included in Bartolomeo Veneto's catalog.

STUDY FOR A SAINT. *Drawing. Florence, Uffizi.* Yashiro, followed by Bertini, accepted the drawing as a study for one of the saints in the Florence *Coronation* (plate 42). Berenson declared it as the work of a follower in Botticelli's Pollaiuolo manner. We certainly would exclude it from Botticelli's oeuvre.

LOCATION OF PAINTINGS

AMSTERDAM

VON RATH COLLECTION
Judith (plate 101).

BARCELONA

CAMBÓ COLLECTION
Portrait of Marullus (plate 62).

BERGAMO

ACCADEMIA CARRARA
The Tragedy of Virginia (plates 102, 104, 106).
Savior (plate 154; attribution).

BERLIN

STAATLICHE MUSEEN
Madonna and St John the Baptist and St John Evangelist (plates 20–22).
Drawings for the Divine Comedy (plates 78–80).
Portrait of a Young Woman (plate 128; attribution).
Venus (plate 131a; attribution).

BOLOGNA

PRIVATE COLLECTION
Angel, drawing (plate 50).

BOSTON

ISABELLA STEWART GARDNER MUSEUM
The Tragedy of Lucretia (plates 103, 107–110).
Nativity (plate 140; attribution).
MUSEUM OF FINE ARTS
Madonna and Child with St John the Baptist (plate 142; attribution).

BRUSSELS

BAUTIER COLLECTION
Lamentation (plate 150; attribution).

CAMBRIDGE

FITZWILLIAM MUSEUM
Adoration of the Magi, fragments (plates 71b–73).
FOGG ART MUSEUM
Mystic Crucifixion (plate 119).
Savior (attribution).

CINCINNATI

EDWARDS COLLECTION
Madonna and Child with St John and an Angel (plate 133b; attribution).

DARMSTADT

KUPFERSTICHKABINETT
The Faithless and the Descent of the Holy Ghost, drawing (plate 99).

DRESDEN

GEMÄLDEGALERIE
Madonna and Child with St John the Baptist (plate 52).
Miracles of St Zenobius (plate 125).

EDINBURGH

NATIONAL GALLERY OF SCOTLAND
Madonna and Child with St John the Baptist (plate 28).

FLORENCE

CORSINI GALLERY
Madonna and Child with Angels (plate 146b; attribution).
PITTI PALACE
Madonna and Child with St John the Baptist (plate 63).
UFFIZI GALLERY
Madonna of the Magnificat (plates 1–4).
Birth of Venus (plates 12–19).
St John the Baptist, drawing (plate 23).
Madonna of the Pomegranate (plates 25–27).
St Barnabas Altarpiece (plates 29–33).
Vision of St Augustine, predella (plate 34).
Pietà, predella (plate 35).
Salome, predella (plate 36).
Extraction of the Heart of St Ignatius, predella (plate 37).
Annunciation (plates 38–41).
Coronation of the Virgin (plates 42–45).
St John on Patmos, predella (plate 46a).
St Augustine, predella (plate 46b).
Annunciation, predella (plate 47a).
St Jerome, predella (plate 47b).
The Miracle of St Eligius, predella (plate 48).
Angel, drawing (plate 51).
Pallas, drawing (plate 58).
St Augustine in His Cell (plate 59).
Nativity, drawing (plate 64).
(Unfinished) Adoration of the Magi (plates 70–71a).
Faun, drawing (plate 88).
Calumny (plates 92–98).
St Jerome, drawing (plate 157; attribution).
Study for a Saint, drawing (attribution).

FRANKFURT

STÄDELSCHES KUNSTINSTITUT

Portrait of a Young Woman (plate 127; attribution).

GLASGOW

ART GALLERY AND MUSEUM
Annunciation (plate 113).

GRANADA

CAPILLA DE LOS REYES
Agony in the Garden (plate 112).

GREENVILLE (SOUTH CAROLINA)

BOB JONES UNIVERSITY
Pentecost (plate 148; attribution).

HAMBURG

KUNSTHALLE
Nude Youth, drawing (plate 90).

HANOVER

NIEDERSÄCHSISCHE LANDESGALERIE
Annunciation (plate 100).

LONDON

BRITISH MUSEUM
Faith, drawing (plate 91).
NATIONAL GALLERY
Portrait of a Youth (plate 7).
Mars and Venus (plates 8–11).
Mystic Nativity (plates 114–118).
Vocation of St Zenobius (plates 120–121).
Miracles of St Zenobius (plates 122–123).
Portrait of a Young Woman (plate 130a; attribution).
Angel, reverse side of above (plate 130b; attribution).
Madonna and Child with St John the Baptist (plate 139; attribution).
Madonna and Child (plate 145a; attribution).
Madonna and Child with St John the Baptist (plate 146a; attribution).

MILAN

AMBROSIANA
Madonna of the Pavilion (plates 54–55).
Pallas, drawing (plate 57).
St Thomas, drawing (plate 68).
POLDI-PEZZOLI MUSEUM
Madonna of the Book (plate 5).
Pietà (plates 66–67).
Coronation of the Virgin (plate 159; attribution).

MONTELUPO (FLORENCE)

CHURCH OF SAN GIOVANNI
Madonna and Child with Four Saints, predella (attribution).

MUNICH

ALTE PINAKOTHEK
Pietà (plate 65).

NEW YORK

BACHE COLLECTION
Coronation of the Virgin, with Four Saints (plate 49).
DUVEEN COLLECTION
Tondo of the Madonna and Child with St John (plate 155a; attribution).
Madonna and Child (plate 156; attribution).
KNOEDLER GALLERIES
Spring (plate 137a; attribution).
Summer (plate 137b; attribution).
Autumn (plate 138a; attribution).
Winter (plate 138b; attribution).
LEHMAN COLLECTION
Annunciation (plate 56).
METROPOLITAN MUSEUM OF ART
The Last Communion of St Jerome (plate 69).
Miracles of St Zenobius (plates 124, 126).
PIERPONT MORGAN LIBRARY
Fragment of the Adoration of the Magi (plate 72).

ROCKEFELLER COLLECTION
Madonna and Child with St John the Baptist (plate 141; attribution).

OTTAWA

NATIONAL GALLERY OF CANADA
Jesus and St John the Baptist (plate 134a; attribution).

PARIS

LOUVRE
Miracle of St John the Evangelist (plate 111).
Portrait of a Boy (plate 134b; attribution).
MUSÉE JACQUEMART-ANDRÉ
Flight Into Egypt (plate 153; attribution).

PHILADELPHIA

MUSEUM OF ART
Portrait of Lorenzo Lorenzano (plate 61).

ROME

BORGHESE GALLERY
Madonna and Child with St John and Angels (plate 144; attribution).
COLONNA GALLERY
Madonna and Child (plate 145b; attribution).
LAZZARONI COLLECTION
Madonna and Child with St John the Baptist (plate 6).
Portrait of a Man (attribution).
PALLAVICINI COLLECTION
The Derelitta (plate 89).
Transfiguration with St Ambrose and St Augustine (plate 147; attribution).

TURIN

GALLERIA SABAUDA
Venus (plate 132; attribution).

VATICAN CITY

VATICAN ART GALLERY
St Sebastian (plate 149; attribution).
VATICAN LIBRARY
Drawings for the Divine Comedy
(plates 74–76).

VIENNA

AKADEMIE DER KUNST
Madonna and Child with Angels (plate 143; attribution).

WASHINGTON, D.C.

NATIONAL GALLERY OF ART
Portrait of a Youth (plate 24).
Madonna and Child (plate 60).
Madonna Enthroned (plate 151a; attribution).

WILLIAMSTOWN (MASSACHUSETTS)

CLARK MUSEUM
Madonna and Child with St John
(plate 53).

LOCATION UNKNOWN

Drawings for the Divine Comedy, formerly in Berlin, Kupferstich-kabinett (plates 77, 81–86).
Portrait of Dante, formerly in Hatfield, Burns Collection (plate 87).
Portrait of a Young Woman, formerly in Munich, Darnheim Antiques (plate 129a; attribution).
Portrait of a Young Woman, formerly in Richmond, Cook Collection (plate 129b; attribution).
Venus, formerly in Lucerne (plate 131b; attribution).
Madonna and Child, formerly in Berlin, Simon Collection (plate 133a; attribution).
Madonna of the Candles, formerly in

Berlin, Kaiser Friedrich Museum (plate 135; attribution).
Annunciation, formerly in Berlin, Kaiser Friedrich Museum (plate 136; attribution).
Madonna and Child, formerly in Paris, Trotti House (plate 151b, attribution).
Annunciation, formerly in Florence, Corsini Gallery (plate 152a; attribution).
Annunciate Virgin, formerly in Florence, Corsini Gallery (plate 152b; attribution).
Baptism of Christ, formerly in Faenea, Guidi Collection (plate 155b; attribution).
Annunciate Angel, formerly in Leningrad, Hermitage (plate 158a; attribution).
Annunciate Virgin, formerly in Leningrad, Hermitage (plate 158b; attribution).
Madonna and Child, formerly in London, Benson Collection (attribution).
Madonna and Child with St Joseph, formerly in Berlin, Simon Collection (attribution).
Madonna and Child with St John, formerly in Vienna, Lanckoronsky Collection (attribution).
Madonna and Child with St John, formerly in Paris, Dreyfus Collection (attribution).
Noli me tangere and *Resurrection*, cited by Van Marle (attribution).
Christ Crowned with Thorns, formerly in Paris, Lazzaroni Collection (attribution).
The Young Redeemer, formerly in New York, Kleinberger Galleries (attribution).
St Dominick, formerly in Leningrad, Hermitage (attribution).
St Jerome, formerly in Leningrad, Hermitage (attribution).

SELECTED CRITICISM

Sandro di Botticello, an excellent painter, on panels and walls. . . .
His things have a manly air, and they are (done) with utmost
reason and whole proportion.

Ludovico's anonymous agent, around 1485

Having given himself over to that art, he followed and imitated
his teacher so carefully that Fra Filippo became fond of him and
taught him his style, which soon developed to such a degree that
no one would have believed. . . .

In Santo Spirito in Florence, he painted a panel for the Bardi
Chapel, which is worked diligently and carried out well, and there
we find several olive and palm trees done with the greatest
love. . . . In the Church of Ognissanti, he painted a fresco of St
Augustine, which work was highly praised because he had re-
vealed with that portrayal the profound thought and very acute
subtlety which mark persons who are dedicated to the . . .
contemplation of very elevated and difficult matters.

GIORGIO VASARI,
The Lives, 1568

So just what Dante scorns as unworthy alike of heaven and hell,
Botticelli accepts, that middle world in which men take no side in
great conflicts, and decide no great causes, and make great
refusals. He thus sets for himself the limits within which art, un-
disturbed by any moral ambition, does its most sincere and surest
work. His interest is neither in the untempered goodness of
Angelico's saints, nor the untempered evil of Orcagna's *Inferno*;
but with men and women, in their mixed and uncertain condition,
always attractive, clothed sometimes by passion with a character
of loveliness and energy, but saddened perpetually by the shadow

upon them of the great things from which they shrink. His morality is all sympathy; and it is this sympathy, conveying into his work somewhat more than is usual of the true complexion of humanity, which makes him, visionary as he is, so forcible a realist. . . .

I have said that the peculiar character of Botticelli is the result of a blending in him of a sympathy for humanity in its uncertain condition, its attractiveness, its investiture at rarer moments in a character of loveliness and energy, with his consciousness of the shadow upon it of the great things from which it shrinks and that this conveys into his work somewhat more than painting usually attains of the true complexion of humanity. He paints the story of the goddess of pleasure in other episodes besides that of her birth from the sea, but never without some shadow of death in the grey flesh and wan flowers. He paints Madonnas, but they shrink from the pressure of the divine child, and plead in unmistakeable undertones for a warmer, lower humanity.

WALTER PATER,
The Renaissance, 1873

In fact, the mere subject, and even representation in general, was so indifferent to Botticelli, that he appears almost as if haunted by the idea of communicating the *unembodied* values of touch and movement. Now there is a way of rendering even tactile values with almost no body, and that is by translating them as faithfully as may be into values of movement. For instance, we want to render the roundness of a wrist without the slightest touch of either light or shade; we simply give the movement of the wrist's outline and the movement of the drapery as it falls over it, and the roundness is communicated to us almost entirely in terms of movement. But let us go one step farther. Take this line that renders the roundness of the wrist, or a more obvious example, the lines that render the movements of the tossing hair, the fluttering draperies, and the dancing waves in the *Birth of Venus*— take these lines alone with all their power of stimulating our imagination of movement, and what do we have? Pure values of movement abstracted, unconnected with any representation whatever. This kind of line then, being the quintessence of movement, has, like the essential elements in all the arts, a power of stimulating our imagination and of directly communicating life. Well! imagine an art made up entirely of these quintessences of movement-values, and you will have something that holds the same relation to representation that music holds to speech—and this art exists, and is called linear decoration. In this art of arts Sandro Botticelli may have had rivals in Japan and elsewhere in the East, but in Europe never. To its demands he was ready to sacrifice everything that habits acquired under Filippo and Pollaiuolo—and his employers!—would permit. The representative element was for him a mere libretto: he was happiest when his subject lent itself to translation into what may be called a linear symphony.

BERNARD BERENSON,
Italian Painters of the Renaissance, 1896

Botticelli was a pupil of Fra Filippo, but that is perceptible only in his very first works. They were of two quite different temperaments: the Frate with his broad laughter and equable, good-humored pleasure in the things of this world, and Botticelli, impetuous, passionate, always inwardly exalted, an artist to whom the painterly qualities of a surface meant little, who found his ideal in linear rhythms and who endowed his heads with a wealth of character and expression. Consider his Madonna with her narrow face, mute mouth, and heavy, troubled eyes; it is quite a different picture from the contented twinkle of Filippo. His Saints are never healthy people with whom all is well, his St Jerome is consumed with inner fire and in the young St John he searches for the expression of fanaticism and asceticism. He takes the holy stories seriously, and this seriousness increases with the years until he abandons all charm of external appearance. His beauty has something afflicted, and even when he smiles it seems only a transitory lighting-up. How little real joy there is in the dance of the Graces in his Primavera, and look what kind of bodies they have! The austere leanness of immaturity has become the ideal of the age; in movement, tension and angularity are sought for rather than the saturated curve, and in every form the stress is on the fine-drawn and pointed, not on the full and rounded.

HEINRICH WÖLFFLIN,
Classic Art, An Introduction to the Italian Renaissance.
Translated by Peter and Linda Murray. London: Phaidon Press

Regarded in its technical aspect, the distinguishing trait of Sandro's art undoubtedly lies in the peculiar and intimate quality of his linear design. Botticelli has been called "a supreme master of the single line"; but a subtler criticism would, I think, prefer to say that among the moderns, he is an unique master of contour, —that he invariably uses his line, to express a definite contour, not only in the outline of the figure, but of some feature, hand, or fold within its mass, and always with a rhythm and beauty of intention which is unparalleled in Florentine art. Ruskin has called Botticelli a "reanimate Greek", and we may re-echo his phrase with a meaning of which he himself, perhaps, was not conscious. In his peculiar rendering of contour, Botticelli came nearer, at least in the technical part of painting, to the literal realization of the ideal of the Renaissance, that new birth of antique art, than any other master of his age.

HERBERT P. HORNE,
Alessandro Filipepi, commonly called Sandro Botticelli. London: George Bell and
Sons, 1908

Supporters of modern movements in Art are crying so much against the imitation of Nature, that there are many cultured people who tend not to approve of a well-finished piece of realistic work, because of its faithful representation of Nature. In the case of Botticelli, appreciative critics began to make much of him as an artist of "presentation" instead of "representation", by which I mean, as an artist of line-function, not dependent upon the representation of Nature. That, I agree, is essentially true of Botticelli, as we shall see. But in their enthusiasm in having discovered the merit of "presentation" almost for the first time in European Art, critics were carried away so far as to imagine that

the appreciation of "presentation" could only be at the expense of
the merit of "representation." These two are logically, and only
logically, incongruous. In human experience they can go side by
side, and in plastic art both of them must exercise their psychic
influences. More than that: in plastic art it is the "representation"
of visual Nature which is indispensable, the requirement of which
differentiates it from other arts, as music and decorative design.
The "presentational" element is directly life-giving, and consti-
tutes a powerful psychological function in Art, but it depends
upon realistic formation for arriving at full, plastic expression.
Botticelli's art was a rare gift in Europe, in the fact that amidst
the too exclusive cult of Realism, he almost alone was capable of
"presentation" in Art, free and ethereal; all the more do I bless
fortune that he was born in an age ardently occupied with what he
by nature lacked, which was indispensable in making him a great
plastic painter. I will show later on, that the most kindred soul to
Botticelli was Utamaro . . .

YUKIO YASHIRO,
Sandro Botticelli. London & Boston: The Medici Society, 1925

Each form becomes, under the painter's hand, poetry. His women
are velvet flowers with their curving lines, their oval pale eyes,
their heads languid under the weight of gold masses. The lined
lights of his sea seem swarms of butterflies. The minute leaves
that wrap around the shrubs still trembling with the winter cold
seem barely to touch them in the portrayals of the earthly paradise.
The exotic charm of the unusual faces, the feverish or languid
rhythm of their bodies create the sense of music . . . Even the
muted tones which Sandro liked so much contribute to the
fascination of his images, despite his love for velvet textures and
glints of gold: pale skies, washed and limpid, water of a tenuous
green, matte roses, and faded rose tones, or velvety browns, olive
flesh, like the early paintings, or grays mixed with silver like the
Birth of Venus . . . The enchanted world of Sandro's art, with
the splendor of his velvet, gold and flower decorations and the
nostalgic charm of his human types and the subtle range of line,

enfolds the dreams of Florence at the dusk of the Quattrocento, on the splendid eve of passionate days that were to be Michelangelo's.

ADOLFO VENTURI,
Botticelli, 1925

What makes Botticelli a unique artist in his time, and lifts him above others, even though they may have been formally more perfect, was not simply his poetic fancy, which Piero di Cosimo possessed not to a lesser degree, even if his forms were less beautiful. Rather it was his sense of proportion between figures and space, in the linear rhythm which links the individual figures and the groups arranged harmoniously in masses, and it was his sense besides of the ideal chromatic delicacy which blends colors with golden highlights. And especially his intimate . . . sensibility, the intense spiritual passion which emanates from his creations . . .

CARLO GAMBA,
Botticelli, 1936

Botticelli puts aside in this painting (*Mystic Nativity*, London) any geometric composition in depth, where the proportions of the figures recede in relation to the distance. Here he fills the canvas like a page from a missal and arranges his figures at different levels. The Virgin dominates them all in size, and is much larger than the figures in the foreground which, according to the norms of linear perspective, should be larger than she. Here the vision is totally symbolic . . . Realism is lacking from the composition, in which the elongated forms are treated with a certain carelessness and indeed rendered awkwardly. We must believe that Botticelli desired the effect, because he was capable of doing otherwise. The faces themselves do not have particular expressions; the feeling is transmitted by the gestures especially—by the line in movement.

This artistic testament . . . reveals the discouragement of a man who takes refuge in a dream. There is no peace on earth for men of good will . . .

J. MESNIL,
Botticelli, 1938

Berenson notes how Botticelli preferred presentation to representation: each element in his paintings—figure or group—is seen by him as a "presence" so immediate that any interest in a coordinated narrative becomes secondary. Venturi adds that the interest in the particular creates the various nuclei of Botticelli's compositions. The intensity with which the detail is felt and realized with its line determines that rhythm of detail which is the secret of Botticelli's art. Venturi's modification makes Berenson's idea critically more concrete and erases the suspicion that had been lurking in the idea of a certain instability in Botticelli's vision (attributed to vacillation or transiency in the artist's feelings). And to dispel the implication that it has been dictated by the modern taste—in the end arbitrary—for anthologizing, it is worthwhile remembering the comment once frequently made: that for Botticelli this isolating of figurative units meant precisely to put the image in focus. The "presentation" of details is a result of the necessity to consolidate the center of the rhythms, to locate the expressive content around central points so that the content would not spend itself simply in imitations of Lippi's descriptive manner. This would have happened had the artist developed the content "horizontally" (and it's relevant here to point out Botticelli's predilection for *tondi*). Therefore, Botticelli is not "fragmentary," a mere maker of motets that in their weariness are detached from his times. He truly composes, even in the large frescoes in the Sistine Chapel. But the unity of composition of these frescoes does not lie in the classic, ordered balance of perspective planes. Rather it lies in the rhythmic series, which follows even here a . . . lyrical coherence . . . a close pictorial weave, the reverse of which, so to speak, would reveal the outlines of continually developing rhythms.

SERGIO BETTINI,
Botticelli, 1942

Never before had the rhythm of the line and the composition succeeded in exhausting the uneven cadence of song, as it has in these pure visions (two frescoes of the Tornabuoni-Lemmi Villa).

The colors themselves achieve a harmony through subtle blends and dissonances, without any apparent relationship with the space and light. The three Graces, for example, stand weightlessly on the ground, almost still. And if their draperies move with the wind, it's because their nature is heavenly and not earthly. That is, the movement is beautiful in itself, and not because it expresses a gesture or indicates that a breeze is blowing, but because the sudden ruffling or the slow unfurling express analogously the alternate and continuous motion of the soul. It becomes the abstract symbol of spirituality.

But just at the point at which the line seems to free itself from the human figure to translate the movement, the abstract rhythm suddenly gives up its secret and offers itself directly to our senses and becomes immediately visible and tangible. It is the line, then, that in its apparent abstraction takes on the concrete, determined and constant value of the form. In fact, the image has now over-come the bonds which held it to the sensible world and no longer emerges from the spiritualization of the object or from an overt search for pure ideas, because the idea itself can be manifest in tangible signs, without losing any of its spirituality. It is the idea, finally, that clearly reveals "beauty," or the particular characteristic of the image. Thus we can say that these two frescoes, these two visions, mark the culminating moment of Botticelli's Neo-Platonism, which will never be surpassed. Beyond this limit, there could no longer exist aspirations or intellectual tensions. There remained the burning fire of faith; certainly Savonarola's sermons contributed, but it was also the logical conclusion of Botticelli's development. And besides, the first signs begin to be felt (much before the crucial moment) of the political and religious struggle between Savonarola and the Medicis.

GIALIO CARLO ARGAN,
Botticelli, 1956

BIBLIOGRAPHICAL NOTE

The Botticelli bibliography is vast, even if for the most part digressive and elementary. In the comments on each work, I have cited just the author's name (followed by the date of publication, when there existed the possibility of confusion) for the monographs that are considered most important critically. They are, beginning with the earliest, H. ULMANN's (*Sandro Botticelli*, Munich, 1893), which, as a philological study, was notable for its time; H. HORNE's (*Alessandro Filipepi, commonly called Sandro Botticelli*, London, 1908), very ample and fundamental for historical research, scholarly exactness, and reconstruction from contemporary documents; W. BODE's (*Botticelli*, Berlin, 1921, and "Botticelli," in *Klassiker der Kunst*, Stuttgart, 1926), in which the author employs his earlier research into the attributions; A. SCHMARSOW's (*Sandro del Botticello*, Dresden, 1923), interesting for his neo-Gothic interpretation of Botticelli's art; Y. YASHIRO's (*Sandro Botticelli*, London, 1925, and with critical catalog, London, 1929), which delves into the artist's work with great sensibility, even if without an adequate synthesis; A. VENTURI's notable study (*Botticelli*, Rome, 1925), which has many new ideas and attributions; L. VENTURI's very revealing profiles (*Botticelli*, London, 1937, 1947 and 1961); the very ample and informed monograph by C. GAMBA (*Botticelli*, Milan, 1936), in which many problems of chronology and influences are put into focus; J. MESNIL's (*Botticelli*, Paris, 1938), a lively reconstruction of the artist's personality and of his milieu, which also takes advantage of the author's wide research into the records; S. BETTINI's (*Botticelli*, Bergamo, 1942), a very sensitive critical study; finally G. C. ARGAN's (*Botticelli*, Geneva, 1957), which puts forward an intelligent interpretation of Botticelli's art in a Neo-Platonic key. More simply explanatory are the essays by E. STEINMANN (1897 on), G. N. PLUNKETT (1900), A. STREETER (1903), E. GEBHART (1907), A. J. RUSCONI (1907), Y. CARTWRIGHT (1912), C. DIEHL (1906), E. SCHAEFFER (1910), R. SCHNEIDER (1911) and various others we cannot mention for lack of space. I. B. SUPINO's essay (*Sandro Botticelli*, Florence, 1910) contains new material from the records and old documents. Obviously good references are the chapter on Botticelli in A. VENTURI's *Storia dell'arte* (Milan, VII, 1) and the chapter in R. VAN MARLE's *Development of the Italian Schools of Painting* (The Hague, 1931, XII), which has particular value in the study of the artist's school and derivations. On Botticelli as portrait painter, cf. H. T. KROEBER (*Die Einzelporträts des Sandro Botticelli*, Leipzig, 1911) and J. ALAZARD (*Le portrait florentin de Botticelli à Bronzino*, Paris, 1924). On his relationship with the ancient world, cf. E. TIETZE-CONRAT, "Botticelli and the Antique," in *The Burlington Magazine*, 1925, XLVII, and R. SALVINI, "Umanesimo di Botticelli," in *Emporium*, 1943. On the allegory and symbolism of Sandro's paintings, besides the work by Argan already cited, we note the essays by R. WITTKOWER and E. GOMBRICH in the *Journal of the Warburg and Courtauld Institutes*, 1939 and

1945 respectively. On Botticelli's color, the study by N. ALLAN PATILLO in *Art Bulletin*, 1954, is notable. On the drawings, BERNARD BERENSON'S *Florentine Drawings* is classic, but cf. also the more recent folder by BERTINI, "Botticelli," *I grandi maestri del disegno*, Bergamo, 1933. The most complete bibliography, up to 1925, is in the work by Yashiro already cited.

The following is a list of studies that have particular themes, or relevance to the major essays cited in the four parts of *All the Paintings of Botticelli* with only the author's name and date of publication. The list is ordered alphabetically, and each author's essays are ordered chronologically, thus facilitating the reader's selection.

AMMIRATO, *Le famiglie nobili fiorentine*, 1642.
ANGELI, in *Archivio storico dell'arte*, 1896.
ANTONIEWICZ, in *Bulletin of the Academy of Sciences of Cracow*, 1905.
L. BARDI, *L'Imperiale e reale Galleria Pitti*, 1837–42.
E. BATTISTI, in *Le vie d'Italia*, 1954.
BENOIS, *Les Trésors d'art en Russie*, 1901.
BERENSON, in *Gazette des Beaux-Arts*, 1889.
— *ibid.*, 1895.
— *ibid.*, 1899.
— *The Drawings of the Florentine Painters*, 1903.
— in *Rassegna d'arte*, 1905.
— *The Drawings of the Florentine Painters*, 1912.
— *The John G. Johnson Collection*, 1913.
— in *Art in America*, 1922.
— in *Dedalo*, 1924.
— *The Drawings of the Florentine Painters*, 1938.
BERTI and BALDINI, *Filippino Lippi*, 1957.
BOCCHI, *Bellezze di Fiorenza*, 1591.
BODE, in Burckhardt, *The Cicerone*, 1884.
— in *Jahrbuch der preussischen Kunstsammlungen*, 1886.
— *Italienische Bildhauer der Renaissance*, 1887.
— in *Gazette des Beaux-Arts*, 1888.
— in Burckhardt, *The Cicerone*, 1893.
— *Die Sammlung Hainauer*, 1897.
— in *Jahrbuch der preussischen Kunstsammlungen*, 1904.
— *ibid.*, 1906.
— *ibid.*, 1907.
— in Burckhardt, *The Cicerone*, 1910.
BODKINS, in *The Burlington Magazine*, 1933.
BODMER, in *Mitteilungen des Kunsthistorisches Institut*, 1931.
BOECK, in *Rivista d'arte*, 1954.
BOFFITO, *L'eresia di Matteo Palmieri*, 1909.
BRIZIO, in *L'arte*, 1933.
BUDINICH, *Il palazzo ducale di Urbino*, 1904.
BURROUGHS, in *Bulletin of the Metropolitan Museum*, 1911.
E. CALZINI, *Urbino*, 2nd ed., 1899.
CIARANFI FRANCINI, *Galleria Pitti*, 1949.
— *ibid.*, 1956.

COLLOBI RAGGHIANTI, *Mostra di Lorenzo il Magnifico*, 1949.
CONTI, in *L'arte*, 1881.
— *ibid.*, 1882.
COOK, in *L'arte*, 1902.
— *ibid.*, 1908.
CREIZENACH, in *Repertorium für Kunstwissenschaft*, 1898.
CROWE, in *Gazette des Beaux-Arts*, 1886.
CUST, in *Les Arts*, 1907.
DADDI-GIOVANNOZZI, in *Rivista d'arte*, 1934.
D'ANCONA, in *L'arte*, 1917.
DAVIES, *National Gallery Catalogue*. Earlier Italian Schools, 1951.
DE FOVILLE, in *Revue de l'art*, 1911.
— in *Revue numismatique*, 1912.
DEGENHARDT, in *Römisches Jahrbuch für Kunstgeschichte*, 1955.
DELLA PERGOLA, *La Galleria Borghese a Roma*, 1950.
DE RINALDIS, *Catalogo della Reale Pinacoteca di Napoli*, 1928.
— *Catalogo della Galleria Borghese*, 1948.
L. DOREZ, in *Bulletin de la Société française d'Histoire de la medecine*, 1907.
EDE, *Florentine Drawings*, 1926.
EPHRUSSI, in *Gazette des Beaux-Arts*, 1882.
— *ibid.*, 1885–86.
FERRARI, in *Rassegna d'arte*, 1903.
FERRI, in *Bollettino d'arte*, 1909.
FIOCCO, in *The Burlington Magazine*, 1930.
FISCHEL, *Die Sammlung Spiridon*, 1929.
FÖRSTER, in *Jahrbuch der preussischen Kunstsammlungen*, 1887.
FRIEDLÄNDER, *Italienische Schaumünzen*, 1882.
FRIZZONI, in *Archivio storico dell'arte*, 1879.
— *ibid.*, 1888.
— *Arte del Rinascimento*, 1891.
— in *Gazette des Beaux-Arts*, 1896.
— in *Archivio storico dell'arte*, 1899.
— in *L'arte*, 1902.
FROTHINGHAM, in *Journal of the Archeological Institute of America*, 1908.
FRY, in *The Burlington Magazine*, 1926.
— *ibid.*, 1930.
GAMBA, in *Il Marzocco*, April 27, 1930.
— in *Dedalo*, 1930–31.
— in *Bollettino d'arte*, 1932.
— in *Miscellanea Supino*, 1933.
— in *Rivista d'arte*, 1934.
GASPARD, in *Les Arts*, 1906.
GASPARY, *Geschichte der italiensche Literatur*, 1885 and 1888.
GEBHARDT, in *Revue de l'art*, 1908.
GIGLIOLI, in *Rassegna d'arte*, 1921.
GNOLI, in *Archivio storico dell'arte*, 1893.
GOMBRICH, in *Journal of the Warburg and Courtauld Institutes*, 1945.
GOMEZ MORENO, in *Gazette des Beaux-Arts*, 1908.
GOTTSCHEWSKI, *Die Bildnisse der Caterina Sforza*, 1908.
GUIFFREY, in *Les Arts*, 1908.

F. HARCK, in *Archivio storico dell'arte*, 1890.
— in *Repertorium für Kunstwissenschaft*, 1896.
HARTLAUB, *Matteo da Siena*, 1910.
HENDY, in *The Burlington Magazine*, 1932.
HOLMES, in *The Burlington Magazine*, 1918.
HORNE, in *Revue archéologique*, 1901.
— in *The Burlington Magazine*, 1903.
— *ibid.*, 1909–10.
— in *Rassegna d'arte*, 1913.
— in *Bulletin of the Metropolitan Museum*, 1915.
— in *The Burlington Magazine*, 1915–16.
J. KERN, in *Jahrbuch der preussischen Kunstsammlungen*, 1905.
KONODY, in *The Connoisseur*, 1908.
— *The Collection of Viscount Rothermere*, 1932.
KUHNEL, *Botticini*, 1907.
KURZ, in *Old Master Drawings*, 1893.
JACOBSEN, in *Repertorium für Kunstwissenschaft*, 1896.
— in *Archivio storico italiano*, 1897.
JAHNIG, *Die Gemäldegalerie an Dresden*, 1929.
P. JAMOT, in *The Burlington Magazine*, 1920.
F. LABAN, in *Zeitschrift für bildende Kunst*, 1906.
LACLOTTE, *De Giotto à Bellini : les primitifs italiens dans les musées de France*,
1956.
LAFENESTRE, *Florence*, 1900.
LANDSBERGER, in *Zeitschrift für Kunstgeschichte*, 1933.
LANGDON DOUGLAS, in *Art in America*, 1942.
LASAREFF, in *The Burlington Magazine*, 1924.
LESSER, in *The Burlington Magazine*, 1930.
LIPPMANN, in *Jahrbuch der preussischen Kunstsammlungen*, 1883.
— *Zeichningen von Sandro Botticelli zu Dante's Göttliche Komödie*, 1st ed. 1886,
2nd ed. 1896.
LOGAN, in *Revue archéologique*, 1900.
LONGHI, *Piero della Francesca*, 1927.
MEISS, in *The Burlington Magazine*, 1951.
MESNIL, in *Zeitschrift für bildende Kunst*, 1900.
— *Miscellanea d'arte*, 1903.
— in *Revue de l'art*, 1911.
— in *Rassegna d'arte*, 1914.
MEYER, *Zur Geschichte der florentinischen Malerei des XV Jahrhunderts*, 1890.
— in *Jahrbuch der preussischen Kunstsammlungen*, 1891.
MIDDELDORF, *Il mondo antico nel Rinascimento*, 1958.
MORELLI, *Italian Masters in German Galleries*, 1873.
— *Berliner Galerie*, 1896.
— *Kunstkritische Studien über italienischer Malerei. Die Galerien Borghese und Doria
Pamphili in Rom*, Vol. I, 1890 Vol. II, 1893.
— in *Kunstchronik*, 1891–92.
— *ibid.*, 1892–93.
MÜLLER-WALDE, *Leonardo*, 1889.
MÜNTZ, in *Chronique des arts*, 1888.
— in *Archivio storico italiano*, 1897.

NEILSON, *Filippino Lippi*, 1938.
ORTOLANI, *Pollaiuolo*, 1949.
OTTLEY, *Italian School of Design*, 1823.
PALM, in *Gazette des Beaux-Arts*, 1944.
PAULI, *Zeichnungen in der Kunsthalle*, 1927.
PERKINS, in *Rassegna d'arte*, 1905.
PICCOLI, in *The Burlington Magazine*, 1930.
PINI, in Vasari, *Le Vite*, 1845.
PITTALUGA, *Lippi*, 1949.
POGGI, in *L'arte*, 1902.
— in *Miscellanea d'arte*, 1903.
— in *The Burlington Magazine*, 1915–16.
POLLINARI, *Scritti d'arte*, 1890.
POPE-HENNESSY, The Nativity. (No 15 of the Gallery Books.)
POPHAM, *Italian Drawings Exhibition at Burlington House*, 1931.
POPHAM and POUNCEY, *Italian Drawings in the British Museum*, 1950.
POST, in *Art in America*, 1914.
PROCACCI, *Catalogo della Galleria dell'Accademia di Firenze*, 1934, 1936, 1951.
PUDELKO, in *Rivista d'arte*, 1936.
RAGGHIANTI, in *Critica d'arte*, 1938.
— *Miscellanea minore di critica d'arte*, 1946.
— *Catalogo della Mostra di Lorenzo il Magnifico*, 1949.
— in *Critica d'arte*, 1954.
REINACH, *Tableaux inédits*, 1906.
— *Répertoire*, IV, 1918.
J. P. RICHTER, *Italian Art in the National Gallery*, 1883.
— *Lectures on the National Gallery*, 1898.
— *The Mond Collection*, 1910.
— in *Art in America*, 1915.
L. M. RICHTER, in *Zeitschrift für bildende Kunst*, 1913.
E. RIDOLFI, in *Archivio storico italiano*, 1890.
— in *Archivio storico dell'arte*, 1893.
— in *Gallerie nazionali italiane*, 1896.
— *ibid.*, 1898.
ROBINSON, *Catalogue of Drawings, Collection of J. Malcolm*, 1876.
ROSENBERG, in *Zeitschrift für bildende Kunst*, 1883.
RUMOHR, *Italienische Forschungen*, No. 2, 1827.
RUSSOLI, *Poldi-Pezzoli*, 1955.
SABATINI, *Pollaiuolo*, 1944.
SALMI, in *Liburni civitas*, 1938.
— *Piero della Francesca e il Palazzo Ducale d'Urgino*, 1945.
— *Studi artistici urbinati*, 1949.
SALVINI, *Saggi su Filippino Lippi*, 1957.
— in *Encyclopedia of World Art*, 1960.
SANT'AMBROGIO, in *Rassegna d'arte*, 1903.
SCHARF, in *Jahrbuch der preussischen Kunstsammlungen*, 1933.
— *Filippino Lippi*, 1935.
SCHMARSOW, *Melozzo da Forlì*, 1886.
— in *Festschrift z.E. des Zunsthistorisches Institut zu Florenz*, 1897.
SCHÖNBRUNNER and MEDER, *Handzeichnungen . . . aus der Albertina . . .*, 1896.

SCHUBRING, *Cassoni*, 1915, 1923.
F. O. SCHULZE, in *Kunstchronik*, 1880.
SIRÉN, *Dessins et tableaux dans les collections de Suède*, 1902.
— in *The Burlington Magazine*, 1904.
— Catalog of the Auction of the Blakesley Collection at the American Art Gallery of New York, 1914.
— *Loan Exhibition of Italian Primitives*, 1917.
SPIELMANN, in *Revue de l'art*, 1907.
STEINMANN, *Die Sixtinische Kapelle*, 1901.
STILMANN, in *The Century Magazine*, 1890.
STRZYGOWSKI, *Die acht Zeichnungen von Sandro Botticelli . . . in Vatican*, 1887.
THIEME, in *Zeitschrift für bildende Kunst*, 1897–98.
TIETZE-CONRAT, in *The Burlington Magazine*, 1925.
UHDE-BERNAYS, in *Cicerone*, 1913.
VALENTINER, *Early Italian Paintings*, 1926.
VAN MARLE, in *International Studio*, 1928.
A. VENTURI, *La Reale Galleria Pitti*, 1891.
— *Tesori d'arte inediti di Roma*, 1896.
— in *L'arte*, 1902.
— in *Gazette des Beaux-Arts*, 1907.
— in *L'arte*, 1908.
— *ibid.*, 1921.
— *ibid.*, 1922.
— *ibid.*, 1924.
— *ibid.*, 1926.
— *Studi dal vero*, 1927.
L. VENTURI, in *L'arte*, 1912.
— *ibid.*, 1914.
— *La Collezione Gualino*, 1926.
— in *L'arte*, 1931.
— *ibid.*, 1932.
— *Italian Paintings in America*, 1933.
VON HADELN, in *Jahrbuch der preussischen Kunstsammlungen*, 1906.
WAAGEN, *Kunstwerke*, 1837.
— *Treasures of Art in Great Britain*, No. 3, 1854.
— *Treasures. . . . Supplement*, 1857.
— *Die Gemäldgalerie in der K. Hermitage*, 1864.
WARBURG, *Botticellis Geburt der Venus*, 1892.
— *Sandro Botticellis Geburt der Venus und Frühling*, 1893.
— *Gesammelte Schriften*, 1932.
WATERHOUSE, in *The Burlington Magazine*, 1939.
WÄTZOLD, *Die Kunst des Porträts*, 1908.
WELLIVER, *L'impero fiorentino*, 1957.
WICKHOFF, in *Jahrbuch der preussischen Kunstsammlungen*, 1906.
WIND, in *Journal of the Warburg and Courtauld Institutes*, 1940–41.
— in *The Burlington Magazine*, 1950.
WITTKOWER, in *Journal of the Warburg and Courtauld Institutes*, 1939.
YASHIRO, in *The Burlington Magazine*, 1925.
— in *Art in America*, 1927.

REPRODUCTIONS

ACKNOWLEDGEMENT FOR PLATES

B. *Anderson, Rome:* plates 1–3, 5, 15–18, 29, 34–38, 42, 44, 45, 54, 59, 63, 89, 102, 129b, 139, 144–45b, 154. *Mansell-Anderson:* plate 25. *Alinari, Florence:* plates 21, 30, 46, 47, 52, 70, 127, 146b. *Gabinetto Fotografico della Sovrintendenza a¹le Gallerie, Florence:* plates 12–13, 23, 51, 58, 64, 71a, 88, 92–98, 157. *Brogi, Florence:* plates 4, 14, 19, 26, 27, 31–33, 39–41, 43, 55, 152. *National Gallery, London:* plates 7–11, 114–18, 120–23, 130, 146a. *Bildarchiv Foto, Marburg:* plates 20, 22, 143. *National Gallery of Art, Washington:* plates 24, 60, 151a. *Claudio Emmer, Milan:* plates 48, 66, 67. *Metropolitan Museum of Art, New York:* plates 49, 69, 124, 126. *Walter Scansaini, Milan:* plates 57, 68. *Stearn and Sons Ltd, Cambridge:* plates 71b, 73. *Archivi Vaticani:* plates 75, 149. *Gardner Museum, Boston:* plates 103–10 and 140. *Walter Steinkopf, Berlin-Dahlem:* plates 128, 131a. *Staatliche Museen, Berlin:* plates 135, 136. *Knoedler Galleries, New York:* plates 137, 138. *Duveen Brothers, New York:* plates 155a, 156. *Annan, Glasgow:* plate 28. *Clark Museum, Williamstown:* plate 53. *Lehman Collection, New York:* plate 56. *Johnson Art Collection, Philadelphia:* plate 61. *F. Serrra, Barcelona:* plate 62. *Bayerische Staatgemälde-sammlungen, Monaco:* plate 65. *Pierpont Morgan Library, New York:* plate 72. *Kleinhempel Fotowerk-satten, Hamburg:* plate 90. *British Museum, London:* plate 91. *Niedersächsische, Landesgalerie, Hanover:* plate 100. *A y R. Mas, Barcelona:* plate 112. *Art Gallery and Museum, Glasgow:* plate 113. *Fogg Art Museum, Cambridge, Mass.:* plate 119. *Deutsche Fotothek, Dresden:* plate 125. *Art Museum, Cincinnati:* plate 133b. *National Gallery of Canada, Ottawa:* plate 134a. *Archives Photographiques des Monuments Histori-ques de France, Paris:* plate 134b. *Museum of Fine Arts, Boston:* plate 142. *Bob Jones University, Greenville:* plate 148. *Bulloz, Paris:* plate 153. *Museo Poldi-Pezzoli, Milan:* plate 159. *National Gallery, London:* color plate IV (Part 4). Material for the remaining color plates was supplied by *Scala, Florence.*

ST AUGUSTINE
Uffizi, Florence
(*detail of plate 59*)

Plate 61. PORTRAIT OF LORENZO LORENZANO
Philadelphia, John G. Johnson Collection

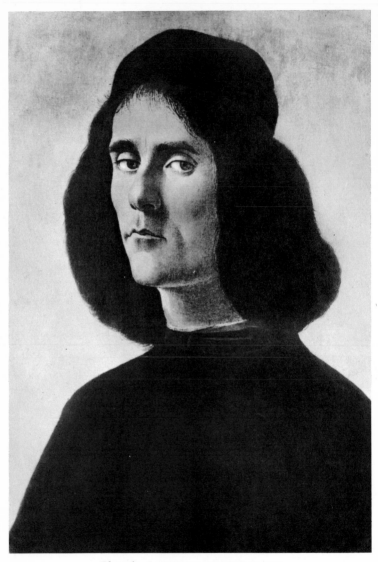

Plate 62. PORTRAIT OF MARULLUS
Barcelona, Cambó Collection

Plate 63. MADONNA AND CHILD WITH ST JOHN THE BAPTIST
Florence, Pitti Palace

Plate 64. NATIVITY
Florence, Uffizi

Plate 65. PIETÀ
Munich, Alte Pinakothek

Plate 66. PIETÀ
Milan, Poldi-Pezzoli Museum

Plate 67. *Detail of plate 66*

Plate 68. ST THOMAS
Milan, Ambrosiana

Plate 69. THE LAST COMMUNION OF ST JEROME
New York, Metropolitan Museum of Art

Plate 70. (UNFINISHED) ADORATION OF THE MAGI
Florence, Uffizi

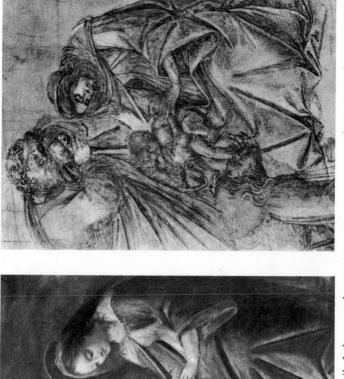

Plate 71. *Detail of plate 70* and ADORATION OF THE MAGI (FRAGMENT)
Cambridge, Fitzwilliam Museum

Plate 72. ADORATION OF THE MAGI (FRAGMENT)
New York, Pierpont Morgan Library

Plate 73. ADORATION OF THE MAGI (FRAGMENT)
Cambridge, Fitzwilliam Museum

Plate 74. CANTO I OF THE INFERNO
Vatican City, Vatican Library

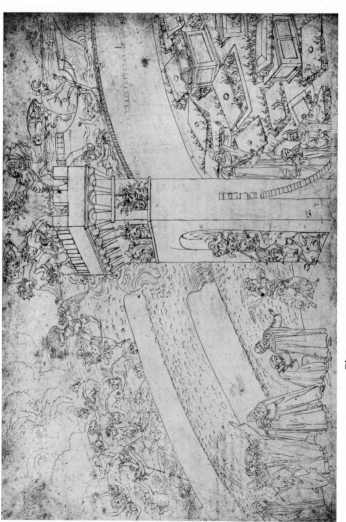

Plate 75. CANTO IX OF THE INFERNO
Vatican City, Vatican Library

Plate 76. CANTO XIII OF THE INFERNO
Vatican City, Vatican Library

CALUMNY
Uffizi; Florence
(*detail of plates 92–93*)

Plate 77. CANTO XXVI OF THE INFERNO
Formerly in Berlin, Kupferstichkabinett

Plate 78. CANTO XXIX OF THE INFERNO
Berlin, Kupferstichkabinett

Plate 79. CANTO XXXI OF THE INFERNO
Berlin, Kupferstichkabinett

Plate 80. CANTO III OF THE PURGATORIO
Berlin, Kupferstichkabinett

Plate 81. CANTO XI OF THE PURGATORIO
Formerly in Berlin, Kupferstichkabinett

Plate 82. CANTO XXXIII OF THE PURGATORIO
Formerly in Berlin, Kupferstichkabinett

Plate 83. CANTO I OF THE PARADISO
Formerly in Berlin, Kupferstichkabinett

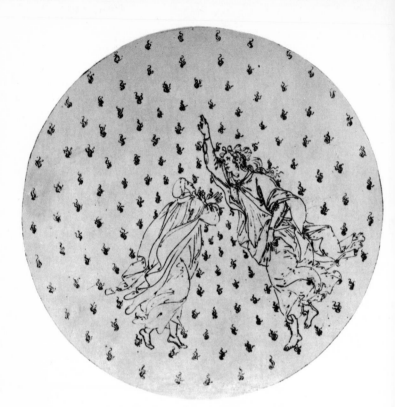

Plate 84. CANTO VI OF THE PARADISO
Formerly in Berlin, Kupferstichkabinett

Plate 85. CANTO XXI OF THE PARADISO
Formerly in Berlin, Kupferstichkabinett

Plate 86. CANTO XXVII OF THE PARADISO
Formerly in Berlin, Kupferstichkabinett

Plate 87. PORTRAIT OF DANTE
Formerly in Hatfield, Burns Collection

Plate 88. FAUN
Florence, Uffizi

Plate 89. LA DERELITTA
Pallavicini Collection, Rome. *Detail*

Plate 90. NUDE YOUTH
Hamburg, Kunsthalle

Plate 91. FAITH
London, British Museum

Plates 92-
Flore

ALUMNY
Uffizi

Plate 94. *Detail of plates 92–93*

Plate 95. *Detail of plates 92–93*

Plate 96. *Details of plates 92–93*

Plate 97. *Detail of plates 92–93*

Plate 98. *Detail of plates 92–93*

Plate 99. THE FAITHLESS AND THE DESCENT OF THE HOLY GHOST
Darmstadt, Kupferstichkabinett

Plate 100. ANNUNCIATION
Hanover, Niedersächsische Landesgalerie

CALUMNY
Uffizi, Florence
(*detail of plates 92–93*)

Plate 101. JUDITH
Amsterdam, Von Rath Collection

Plate 102. TRAGEDY OF VIRGINIA
Bergamo, Accademia Carrara

Plate 103. TRAGEDY OF LUCRETIA
Boston, Isabella Stewart Gardner Museum

Plate 104. *Detail of plate 102*

Plate 105. *Detail of plate 102*

Plate 106. *Detail of plate 102*

Plate 107. *Detail of plate 103*

Plate 108. *Detail of plate 103*

MYSTIC NATIVITY
London, National Gallery
(*detail of plate 114*)

Plate 109. *Detail of plate 103*

Plate 110. *Detail of plate 103*

Plate III. MIRACLE OF ST JOHN EVANGELIST
Paris, Louvre

Plate 112. AGONY IN THE GARDEN
Granada, Capilla de los Reyes

Plate 113. ANNUNCIATION
Glasgow, Art Gallery and Museum

Plate 114. MYSTIC NATIVITY
London, National Gallery

Plate 115. *Detail of plate 114*

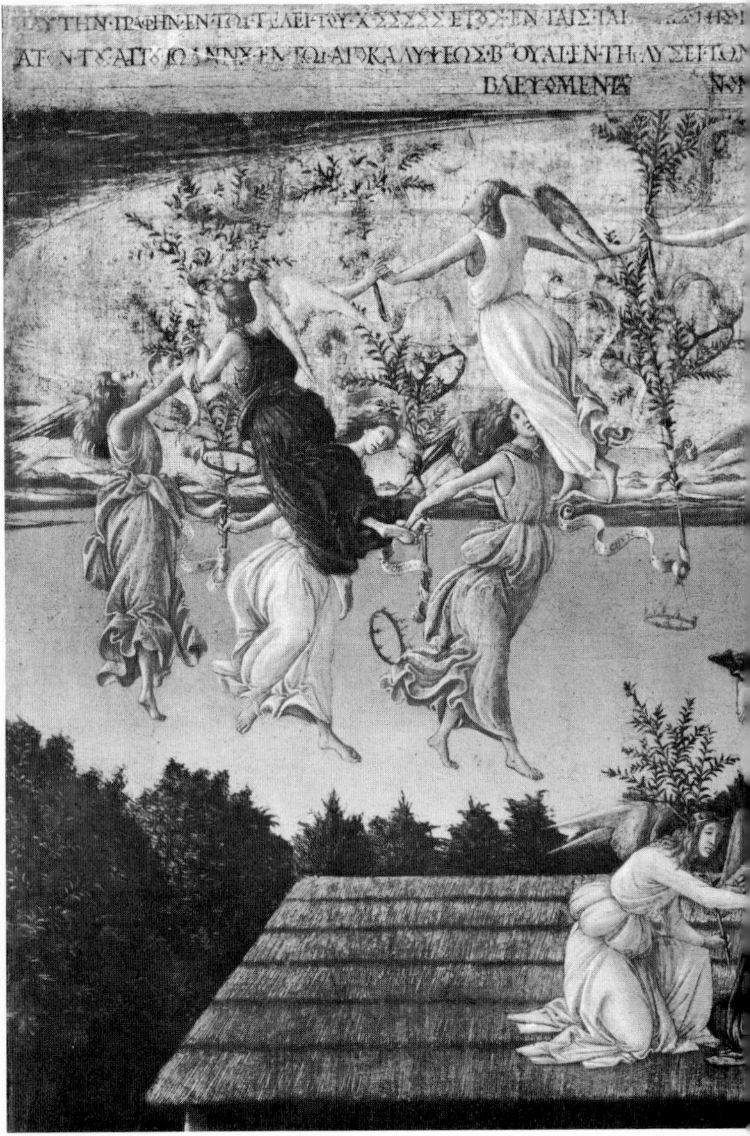

Plates 116–11

ail of plate 114

Plate 118. *Detail of plate 114*

Plate 119. MYSTIC CRUCIFIXION
Cambridge, Massachusetts, Fogg Art Museum

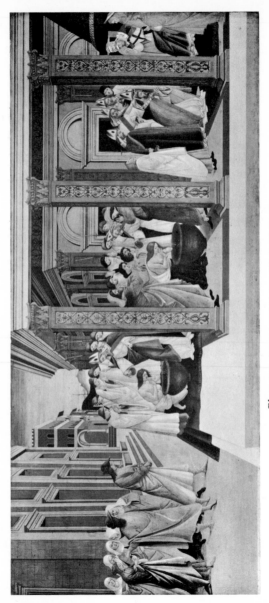

Plate 120. VOCATION OF ST ZENOBIUS
London, National Gallery

Plate 121. *Details of plate 120*

Plate 122. MIRACLES OF ST ZENOBIUS
London, National Gallery

Plate 123. *Details of plate 122*

Plate 124. MIRACLES OF ST ZENOBIUS
New York, Metropolitan Museum of Art

Plate 125. MIRACLES OF ST ZENOBIUS
Dresden, Gemäldegalerie

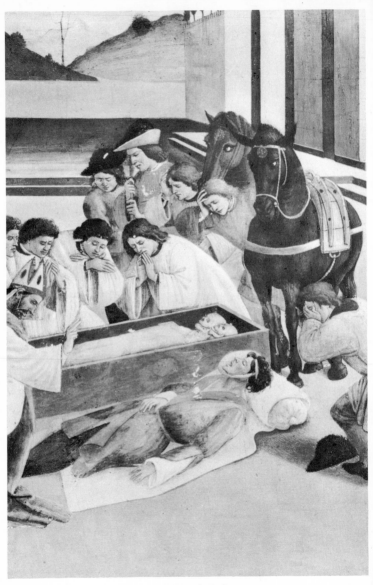

Plate 126. *Detail of plate 124*

ATTRIBUTED WORKS

· Plate 127. PORTRAIT OF A YOUNG WOMAN
Frankfurt, Städelsches Kunstinstitut

Plate 128. PORTRAIT OF A YOUNG WOMAN
Berlin, Staatliche Museen

Plate 129. PORTRAIT OF A YOUNG WOMAN
Formerly in Munich, Bernheim Antiquarian.
Formerly in Richmond, Cook Collection

Plate 130. PORTRAIT OF A YOUNG WOMAN, and on the reverse, AN ANGEL
London, National Gallery

Plate 131. VENUS
Berlin, Staatliche Museen *and*
Formerly in Lucerne, Private Collection

Plate 132. VENUS
Turin, Galleria Sabauda

Plate 133. MADONNA AND CHILD *and* MADONNA AND CHILD, ST JOHN
THE BAPTIST AND AN ANGEL
Cincinnati, Edwards Collection

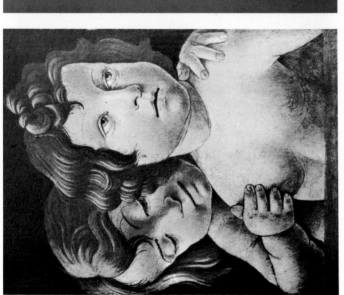

Plate 134. JESUS AND ST JOHN THE BAPTIST *and* PORTRAIT OF A YOUTH
Ottawa, National Gallery of Canada *and* Paris, Louvre

Plate 135. MADONNA OF THE CANDLES
Formerly in Berlin, Kaiser Friedrich Museum

Plate 136. ANNUNCIATION
Formerly in Berlin, Kaiser Friedrich Museum

Plate 137. SPRING and SUMMER
New York, Knoedler Galleries

Plate 138. AUTUMN *and* WINTER
New York, Knoedler Galleries

Plate 139. MADONNA AND CHILD, ST JOHN THE BAPTIST AND AN ANGEL
London, National Gallery

Plate 140. NATIVITY
Boston, Isabella Stewart Gardner Museum

Plate 141. MADONNA AND CHILD WITH ST JOHN THE BAPTIST
New York, John D. Rockefeller Jr. Collection

Plate 142. MADONNA AND CHILD WITH ST JOHN
Boston, Museum of Fine Arts

Plate 143. MADONNA AND CHILD WITH TWO ANGELS
Vienna, Akademie der Kunst

Plate 144. MADONNA AND CHILD WITH ST JOHN AND ANGELS
Rome, Borghese Gallery

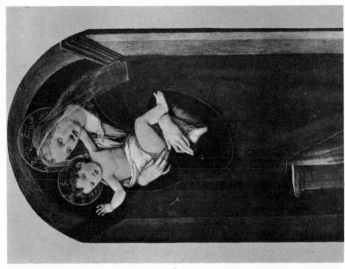

Plate 145. MADONNA AND CHILD
London, National Gallery *and* Rome, Colonna Gallery

Plate 146. MADONNA AND CHILD WITH ST JOHN THE BAPTIST and
MADONNA AND CHILD WITH ANGELS
London, National Gallery *and* Florence, Corsini Gallery

Plate 147. TRANSFIGURATION, WITH SS AMBROSE AND AUGUSTINE
Rome, Pallavicini Collection

Plate 148. PENTECOST
Greenville, South Carolina, Bob Jones University

Plate 149. ST SEBASTIAN
Vatican City, Vatican Museums

Plate 150. LAMENTATION
Brussels, Bautier Collection

Plate 151. ENTHRONED MADONNA and MADONNA AND CHILD
Washington, D.C., National Gallery of Art *and* Paris, Trotti House

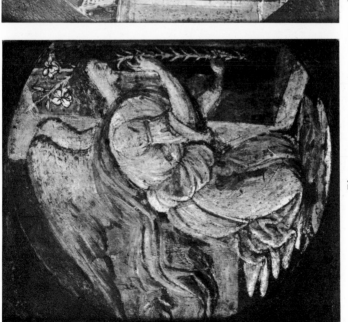

Plate 152. ANNUNCIATE ANGEL and ANNUNCIATE VIRGIN
Formerly in Florence, Corsini Gallery

Plate 153. FLIGHT INTO EGYPT
Paris, Musée Jacquemart-André

Plate 154. REDEEMER
Bergamo, Accademia Carrara

Plate 155. TONDO OF THE MADONNA AND CHILD WITH ST JOHN and
BAPTISM OF CHRIST
New York, Duveen Collection *and* Formerly in Faenza, Guidi Collection

Plate 156. MADONNA AND CHILD
New York, Duveen Collection

Plate 157. ST JEROME
Florence, Uffizi

Plate 158. ANNUNCIATE ANGEL and ANNUNCIATE VIRGIN
Formerly in Leningrad, Hermitage

Plate 159. CORONATION OF THE VIRGIN, WITH FOUR ANGELS AND
TWO WORSHIPPERS
Milan, Poldi-Pezzoli Museum